Industrialization and Political Affinity

This volume looks at the issue of political affinity as a way of explaining industrial policies in Newly Industrializing Countries (NICs). Focusing on Brazil as one of the most technologically and economically advanced of the NICs, Roy Nelson looks at how political affinity can help – or hinder – industrial policies to promote the development of indigenous technological capabilities within NICs. He looks at the ways in which democratization can affect the abilities of these countries to make and implement effective policies for development. The book concludes with some observations on what kind of models for industrial development might be most appropriate in light of the issues raised.

The discussion calls into question the prevailing emphasis of the democratization literature on continued top-down modes of government in post-transition regimes, particularly in Latin America. The volume will be of great value to scholars interested in development and democratization as well as to policymakers involved with NICs.

Roy C. Nelson is Assistant Professor of International Studies at Thunderbird, the American Graduate School of International Management (AGSIM) in Glendale, Arizona, USA.

Thunderbird Routledge series in international management

The American Graduate School of International Management, Thunderbird, focuses on global business education. Combining strengths in all the key areas of international management, it provides a multicultural and multilingual approach to doing business worldwide.

The series presents a range of books which look at the various aspects of international management. Its breadth of coverage ranges from cultural analyses for effective management practice to key issues in world business. Designed to represent the variety of the work undertaken by the school at all levels, whether research into specific topics, textbooks in core business functions, or books directed to the thinking manager, the overall aim is to present the importance of international management issues to an international audience.

Industrialization and Political Affinity

Industrial Policy in Brazil

Roy C. Nelson

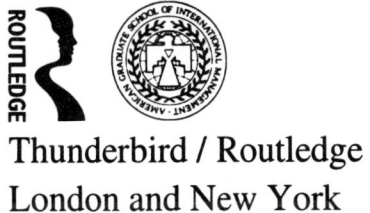

Thunderbird / Routledge

London and New York

First published 1995
by Routledge
11 New Fetter Lane London EC4P 4EE

Simultaneously published in the USA and Canada
by Routledge
29 West 35th Street, New York, NY 10001

© 1995 Roy C. Nelson

Typeset in Times by Michael Mepham, Frome, Somerset
Printed and bound in great Britain by
Mackays of Chatham PLC, Chatham, Kent

British Library Cataloguing in Publication Data
A catalogue record for this book is available from the British Library

Library of Congress Cataloguing in Publication Data
A catalogue record for this book has been requested

ISBN 0–415–12528–6

To my Mother

Contents

Acknowledgements

I am grateful to many people who have helped me in the process of writing this book.

Peter Katzenstein, the chairman of my doctoral committee at Cornell University, guided me through the first incarnation of the book as a Ph.D. dissertation for the Department of Government at Cornell. Peter's thorough, challenging comments were enormously helpful, and his high standards encouraged me always to do my best. I feel very lucky indeed to have had him as a mentor during my graduate school years. Jonas Pontusson and Eldon Kenworthy also provided constructive comments at important stages in the writing process.

At Thunderbird, Llewellyn Howell, Chairman of the Department of International Studies, has helped to provide an "operating environment" supportive of scholarly endeavor that I have found to be tremendously inspirational and conducive to productivity. My colleagues in the Department – and indeed in the entire school, with its broad international focus – have made Thunderbird an extremely stimulating and enjoyable place in which to work.

Family and friends have been supportive throughout the long and challenging process of bringing this book to completion. My parents, especially, provided a great deal of encouragement. Most of all, I am grateful that they valued and appreciated what I was doing. My brothers, Michael and Bill, and my grandmother, gave encouragement that only close family members can give. I would also like to thank those who have been my close friends during this time: Steve Gassner, Keith Brandt, and Margie Casagrande. Finally, Sally Willis of the CAPS center at Thunderbird deserves mention for her assistance in setting the typescript of the book in the proper format.

1 Introduction

Among other important current issues that face the world today, one of the most dramatic is the effort by Newly Industrializing Countries (NICs) to transcend dependent, underdeveloped status and join the ranks of the developed nations. A central aspect of this effort is the implementation of policies to acquire indigenous technological capabilities.[1] This endeavour is occurring simultaneously with another phenomenon among the NICs, the trend toward democratization and the consolidation of fragile democratic regimes. Among the questions this book seeks to answer is, can the NICs successfully accomplish both tasks at the same time? How will democratization affect the abilities of the NICs to make industrial policies for the promotion of development?

In Brazil perhaps more clearly than anywhere else, these issues are central to what is happening now and what will determine the course of the future. One of the most technologically and economically advanced of the NICs, Brazil went through a long process of democratization in the 1980s. This process resulted in the transition from military to civilian rule in 1985 and a direct presidential election (the first in 25 years) in 1989. Brazil thus provides a highly favorable setting in which to study these issues at first hand.

During the military regime, Brazil's leaders put great effort into increasing the country's technological capabilities. Seeking to improve or at least maintain Brazil's economic position *vis-à-vis* the developed nations, the military leaders nurtured and promoted many high-technology sectors, including such industries as computers, nuclear power, and aircraft. Using a broadly construed notion of national security as justification for these efforts, the government provided high levels of political support for each of these industries during the military years. With democratization, however, and the focus of the rising democratic opposition politicians on the social needs of the population, such efforts were less justifiable on these broad "national security" grounds. The question arises: would the new, civilian politicians maintain high levels of government political support for these industries?

Looking at the period leading up to and after the recent transition to civilian rule in Brazil, we find that there is an interesting puzzle which is very relevant to this question, and which touches on both of the major themes we raised at the outset. During this period, supporters of the computer industry had remarkable success in maintaining government support for their programs, while those in the pharmaceutical sector did not – in fact, quite the opposite.

What makes these widely divergent outcomes so puzzling is that they appear to contradict intuitive ideas about how "transitions to democracy" might be expected to affect industrial policy in a NIC such as Brazil. In order to understand this, one needs to understand, first, the extent of the hostility on the part of the incoming civilian politicians toward any policy perceived to be closely linked to the outgoing military regime – as the military regime's computer policy, with its strong emphasis on development of computer technology for "national security" reasons, certainly was. Indeed, in the late 1970s, important civilian (opposition) politicians had expressed fierce antagonism toward the government's computer policy because of what they perceived to be its potential for serving militaristic purposes. Thus, given this political context (to be discussed more fully in Chapters 2 and 3), one would expect that with the shift from military to civilian rule, political support for the "national security"-oriented computer industry would decline, or (because of the military's enduring presence) at best stay the same.

Moreover, by the mid-1980s the military government itself was already seeking to pull back from its strong political support for the computer industry, for the purely technocratic, economically rational reason that the protectionist computer policies were proving to be too inefficient. In particular, other industrial sectors were being hurt by the policy. Nevertheless, the new civilian government actually *increased* government support for the policy, disregarding the absence (by this time) of a clear-cut economic rationale for such action.

Thus, the very strong support for this industry, during the democratic transition period, on the part of the very same civilian politicians who had opposed it so vehemently just a few years before, is surprising. So, too, is the *lack* of support from these politicians during this period for the "social"-oriented pharmaceutical sector, given the determination of the civilian policymakers to focus more government attention on social concerns, and their tendency to see the pharmaceutical industry as associated with such matters.[2]

Is there some pattern in these puzzling outcomes? And does it apply more broadly to high-tech industrialization in NICs undergoing democratization? In seeking to answer such questions, this book examines government policy during the transition and after toward the Brazilian computer and pharmaceutical industries. The specific question this book seeks to answer is, why have supporters of Brazil's computer industry had relative success in maintaining high levels of government support for their programs, while those working within the national pharmaceutical industry have experienced primarily defeat?[3]

OVERVIEW OF THE ARGUMENT

My explanation for these counterintuitive outcomes centers on the *political* characteristics of what I call the *corpo técnico* of each of these sectors.[4] *Corpo técnico* is the term I use to refer to a broad coalition of scientists, industrialists, and technically trained government bureaucrats within a given high-tech industry. My argument is that *corpos técnicos* in different sectors have different political orientations. As a result, depending on the political orientation of the dominant political party or coalition, some *corpos técnicos* will have a stronger "political affinity"[5] than others with that party or coalition. This stronger affinity will make these *corpos técnicos* more successful in promoting policies favorable to their interests. Moreover, members of the *corpo técnico*, whose skills are essential to the viability of any high-tech sector, will be more willing and enthusiastic participants in programs and policies developed in cooperation with a sympathetic political elite.

For the Brazilian case, my argument is that in the process of the transition from the rightist military regime to the (relatively!) left-of-center, PMDB-dominated civilian regime, the political characteristics of the computer *corpo técnico* – much more so than those of the pharmaceutical *corpo técnico* – became more in harmony with the political characteristics of those in power. In this particular instance, the dominant political actor was the PMDB party.[6] As the political affinity of the computer *corpo técnico* and the dominant political party increased, it brought about high levels of renewed support for the computer industry – a sector for which, under the previous regime, political support had been declining. Because the political affinity of the pharmaceutical *corpo técnico* and the dominant political party was relatively low, political support for the pharmaceutical sector, after a brief increase, dwindled.

This, of course, is a somewhat oversimplified version of what brought about these particular outcomes. In fact, such outcomes were the result of a causal chain of variables, as shown in Figure 1.1.

| Foreign ownership and technological dominance | → Access → Political affinity → Policy → Economic outcomes |

Figure 1   The overall model

In Figure 1.1 "foreign ownership and technological dominance" refers to the extent of foreign ownership of a given sector and the extent to which foreign firms control the technology associated with a given sector (i.e., the technology required for manufacturing computer or pharmaceutical products). As the chart indicates, this variable influences whether the *corpo técnico* will be able to have political "access" to policymakers. If the level of foreign ownership and technological dominance is too high, efforts on the part of a *corpo técnico* to influence the policymaking process are likely to be rebuffed and fail; indeed, such efforts are less likely even to occur. Yet access alone does not guarantee that the political outcomes (i.e., "policy") the *corpo técnico* seeks will happen. The *corpo técnico* must also have sufficient "political affinity" with the dominant party or coalition in the government. If sufficient political affinity exists, then the political outcomes the *corpo técnico* wishes to obtain can result, and these, in turn, can be one of many factors determining economic outcomes.[7]

While this overall model encompasses many variables, the focus of this book is on political affinity, a variable which plays a particularly important role during times of democratic transition. Before going on to a more thorough discussion of political affinity, however, we need to take a closer look at "foreign ownership and technological dominance" and "access," those factors which precede political affinity in the model.

While similar in their high degree of technological sophistication, the computer and pharmaceutical industries made use of different kinds of technology. These differences, along with the different timing in the intro-duction of these technologies, resulted in different levels of foreign ownership and technological dominance in the Brazilian computer and pharmaceutical industries.

Technological factors and timing favored national ownership in the com-puter industry. The development of microprocessor technology in the computer industry in the 1970s meant that most of the electronic technology needed for producing mini- and microcomputers – rapidly becoming the most dynamic component of the computer market worldwide – could now be put into very dense integrated circuits and microprocessors, and placed on silicon chips. As Tigre points out, "[s]ince such devices [microprocessors] can be purchased from independent suppliers, small new firms with ingenious design teams achieved tremendous success developing products incorporating the new technology " (Tigre 1983:4). Making use of this now more readily available fundamental technological building block in computer manufacture, new firms, including those in Brazil, could go on to design and produce their own computers.

Timing worked to the advantage of the Brazilian computer sector as well. In the early 1970s, the foreign computer firms had not yet come to dominate the Brazilian computer market. In part because of this fact, the government, over the course of the 1970s, was able to develop a policy of restricting foreign firms' abilities to import computers into the Brazilian market as well as to manufacture them in Brazil. This was the "market reserve"[8] policy for computers, which reserved the Brazilian market for small and medium-sized computers for Brazilian firms alone.

Given these favorable technological and timing factors, domestic firms, by 1986, made up 90 percent of all computer firms in the country (Latin American Development Bank 1988:137). This high level of national ownership facilitated political access on the part of the computer *corpo técnico* during the democratic transition. Lacking a strong foothold in the Brazilian economy, the foreign firms were not able to exert sufficient political pressure to prevent Brazilian politicians from backing policies to support the national computer industry.

In the pharmaceutical industry, the technology and timing factors were not as favorable. With regard to technology, extensive research and development went into the production of the necessary primary ingredients for the making of new drugs. The process was both lengthy and expensive. Indeed, "the discovery, development and introduction of a new primary ingredient took on the average 7 to 10 years... and cost in the range of US$10 million dollars, of which about two-thirds went for basic research and one-third for development" (Kupfert 1985:4).

In addition, the timing factor discouraged domestic political support for an indigenous pharmaceutical industry. The foreign firms had developed technological capabilities relatively early (partly as a result of the development of antibiotics in World War II) and had had time – beginning in the 1940s and 1950s – to dominate the Brazilian pharmaceutical market. The Brazilian government, not as attuned at that time as it would be later to problems of denationalization, failed to establish policies that could prevent this phenomenon from occurring. By the 1980s, when the pharmaceutical *corpo técnico* began proposing serious efforts to promote indigenous technological development in this sector, the government was unable to prevail over the political pressures from the TNCs.

Thus, while joint ventures and wholly Brazilian-owned firms made up over 80 percent of total firms in the pharmaceutical sector, nationally owned firms held (in terms of sales) only 17 percent of the market; the TNCs held the rest (Gerez, Pedrosa 1987:15). This high level of foreign ownership impeded political access on the part of the pharmaceutical *corpo técnico*. The TNCs in this sector had become so strong and well-established that politicians were disinclined to oppose them.

In the pharmaceutical sector, then, political access was low; in computers, in contrast, political access was (relatively) high. These varying degrees of access determined the extent to which the political affinity variable could function. In the computer industry, this variable had the potential to have a great deal of influence. While politicians and other policymakers during the transitional period were not necessarily in favor (originally) of proposals to increase government political support for the computer industry, they did not immediately overrule such proposals. Thus, the high degree of political affinity between the computer *corpo técnico* members advancing such pro-posals, and the new democratic opposition politicians coming to power, was able to play itself out to the fullest.

In the pharmaceutical industry, in contrast, the extent of the political affinity variable's potential influence was more limited. During the demo-cratic transition and afterward, policymakers were already predisposed to be against measures advocating an increase in government political support for the pharmaceutical industry. Thus, the pharmaceutical *corpo técnico* mem-bers – most of whom did not have a high degree of political affinity with those coming into power in any case – did not even have as much potential to benefit from the political affinity variable as did their counterparts in the computer industry.

Despite all of these qualifications, however, the political affinity variable – as the case studies will demonstrate – significantly altered the course of the Brazilian government's industrial policy. Without the influence of the politi-cal affinity factor, the government's support for the computer industry would almost certainly have declined after the transition to democratic rule in the mid-1980s, and programs to support the pharmaceutical industry would at least have had a fighting chance to succeed.

To illustrate the way political affinity works, a brief discussion of the means of recruitment into the various *corpos técnicos*[9] is instructive. (Of course, in analyzing such "recruitment," one must keep in mind that it was not planned or determined formally, by outside authorities. Rather, it resulted from a process of self-selection.)

The computer *corpo técnico* – electronics engineers, entrepreneurs with technical background in computers, technically trained government officials – tended to be young, ambitious, well-educated, and highly intelligent individuals from middle-class families. The computer sector attracted such people because in Brazil, as elsewhere, it had an aura of excitement and promise that other, more traditional fields could not offer. Significantly, this "best and the brightest" segment of the Brazilian population overwhelmingly held political views that, by Brazilian standards at least, were to the left of center. Advocating, among other things, direct elections for president and a greater governmental concern for social welfare, key individuals in this group aligned themselves with Brazil's main opposition movement, the *Movimento Democrático Brasileiro* (MDB), which later became the opposition party (PMDB).

People working within the pharmaceutical industry were different from those in the computer field. Pharmaceuticals had never been identified with the kind of excitement, even glamour, with which computers were associated. This was true even before the transnational corporations dominated the Brazilian market. Nothing like the tremendous, widespread degree of publicity and enthusiasm that the computer industry enjoyed in the 1960s and 1970s had ever hit the pharmaceutical sector. Local pharmaceutical companies had existed in Brazil for decades and still produced mainly basic, traditional products like elixirs or salves. Ownership and the operation of many of these firms was maintained within one family and passed on from generation to generation. Perhaps partly as a result of this, management of these firms was often weak, risk-averse, and inefficient. These aspects of the industry kept it from being attractive to the best graduates of the universities, the ones who, incidentally, were the most articulate and active in their opposition to the military regime.

This difference in the character of the two industries was an important factor in determining government policy, and especially so both during and after the transition to civilian rule. Given its particular political stance, the computer *corpo técnico* – unlike the pharmaceutical *corpo técnico* – found natural allies in the PMDB. In earlier years leftist members of the computer *corpo técnico* had often found themselves in the uncomfortable position of developing technology in cooperation with military personnel, or devising government programs to promote the industry under the auspices of the military. In such cases, both sides worked together toward their common goal but remained suspicious of each other. The compatibility of the computer *corpo técnico*'s views with the PMDB, however, which with the transition was to become the dominant party, allowed for a high degree of mutual trust and cooperation. This facilitated the computer *corpo técnico*'s lobbying efforts.

Increasing opposition to the market reserve from other industrial sectors, and the natural antipathy on the part of civilian leaders toward policies long associated with the military regime, meant that without this special ability to lobby the PMDB, the computer *corpo técnico* would soon have received greatly diminished support from the government. Thus, contrary to all expectations, high post-transition levels of support for policies the computer *corpo técnico* favored went beyond what the military itself would have sought. Clearly, in order to support such policies, the new government was willing to pay a very heavy price. It was willing to antagonize other domestic industrial sectors which had to go without the relatively cheaper, higher quality computers available on the international market. And it was also willing – precisely at the moment when the new government was preparing to undertake negotiations on the foreign debt – to irritate Brazil's major creditor, the United States (which strongly opposed the market reserve). The government's increased support for the computer sector at this particular time, then, underscores just how powerful the influence of the political affinity variable was.

THE ARGUMENT IN THEORETICAL CONTEXT

Dependency theory in general has come under heavy criticism in the last decade.[10] Although in some ways the questions this book addresses touch on issues relevant to the dependency literature, my theoretical approach is in fact quite different. My analysis has its basis in the literature on bargaining theory (as I will explain further below), in the literature on authoritarianism, and in the rapidly growing literature on redemocratization.

The now *passé* "orthodox," or traditional, versions of dependency theory emphasized the way in which international economic domination imposes constraints on development on the less developed countries (Frank 1967). Dependency theory – even in its most sophisticated formulations – goes too far in arguing that these constraints can never be overcome within the context of the capitalist system. Certainly, however, there is some validity to the argument that the domination of certain sectors and markets by TNCs creates difficulties for local firms in less developed countries. Put in the terminology of this book, we might say that a high level of foreign ownership and technological dominance results in a low degree of access for the *corpo técnico*.

What the conventional dependency theory neglected, however, was the role in the policymaking process of domestic forces within Third World countries themselves. Some of the more recent and sophisticated work in the dependency paradigm, as well as in the "bargaining school" which arose in reaction to that paradigm,[11] has attempted to make up for this deficiency. This recent work puts great emphasis on the role of domestic forces in accounting for various levels of success in developing technologically innovative industries in NICs such as India, Mexico, and Brazil (Grieco 1984; Gereffi 1983; Bennett, Sharpe 1985).

While others, then, have considered the effects of domestic politics on an NIC's ability to overcome high levels of foreign control, most of these studies tend to focus on one industrial sector, and suffer from the theoretical inadequacies such limitations create. Moreover, the emphasis throughout these studies tends to be not so much on domestic *politics*, as it is on the domestic political *structure* of the NICs. An analysis that explains an NIC's industrial policies on the basis of the strength of its domestic structure may have the virtue of being highly parsimonious. But as outcomes in the Brazilian case indicate, explanations that take into account such factors as the political orientation of a given regime's dominant political coalition, and the extent to which that orientation corresponds to the political characteristics of various industrial sectors – i.e., political affinity – may be more accurate.

In any case, more is clearly needed to explain varying outcomes in different industrial sectors. Peter Evans's 1979 work, *Dependent Development: The Alliance of Multinational, State, and Local Capital in Brazil*, while written earlier than many others that focus on domestic factors, does attempt to deal with this problem (Evans 1979). It examines many industrial sectors and provides a general explanation to account for the Brazilian state's bargaining power for those sectors in relation to transnational corporations. Yet the argument Evans makes in this early work, that the Brazilian government will not prevail over the TNCs in industries characterized by rapid technological change and innovation, would seem to conflict with later events. Specifically, the initial development of computer industries – which were certainly undergoing rapid technological change and innovation – in India and Brazil appeared to contradict Evans's views. The question remained as to whether these industries would endure; this is an issue we will discuss further below. But Evans's early arguments seemed unable to account even for the initial policies that brought these industries into existence in the first place.

One alternative explanation to account for the emergence of a computer industry in Brazil, advanced by Emanuel Adler, was that ideological factors, and the presence of a highly motivated technological elite, were crucial in bringing about the "success" of Brazil's computer industry.[12] Highly trained electronics engineers and computer scientists, frustrated about not being able to use their talents to the full extent in their home country and firmly committed to the belief that technological dependence is something that can and should be overcome, persuaded the political elite to follow policies to create a local computer industry. Because of the strength of the ideological element in motivating these individuals, as well as their persistence and zeal, Adler referred to them as "ideological guerrillas."

Adler's analysis is useful for a number of reasons. For one thing, it moves away from the domestic structure argument to consider other kinds of domestic forces operating within an NIC. Moreover, it focuses attention on the importance of highly trained engineers, computer scientists, etc. – in Portuguese, *técnicos*, i.e., those with advanced technical training in a given area – in the formation of policy. These individuals are indeed crucial in the early phases of the development of policies to foster high-tech development. Yet in some ways Adler's explanation is seriously deficient. First (in contrast to the recent dependency and bargaining school explanations), it does not adequately take into account the importance, in the making of industrial policy, of the government's independence from the pressures exerted by TNCs. The "strong domestic structure" explanations, which we have just finished criticizing, *do* consider such factors. The error of such explanations lies not in their pointing out the importance of state autonomy from the TNCs, but in focusing on this variable to the exclusion of others that might be just as important, if not more so – e.g., a shift in political regime. Second, because of the limited time-frame of his analysis, Adler does not deal with the issue of how the *técnicos* can *maintain* the policies favorable to the industries after these policies have been created. Thus Adler neglects to consider the impact on industrial policy of a major change in the political regime. This factor, especially relevant now as NICs throughout Latin America and elsewhere experience a democratizing trend, is significant because it can bring about critical changes in the nature of the political elite the *técnicos* are trying to persuade.

This second problem with Adler's argument deserves some further discussion, not only because it is important in itself, but because it demonstrates just how different Adler's argument is from my own. In this book, the *political* characteristics of the *corpo técnico*,[13] as well as the *political* characteristics of the politicians the *corpo técnico* lobbies, are fundamentally important in determining outcomes. For instance, Adler's approach overlooks the significance of the relatively democratic political inclinations of the computer *corpo técnico*, and how this affects its ability to interact with particular members of the political regime in power at any given time.

Evans, in an attempt to defend and modify his own earlier ideas, points out how Adler's slighting of the importance of the government's independence from the political pressures of foreign firms presents difficulties for Adler's explanation of the Brazilian computer case (Evans 1986:791– 808). The Brazilian computer industry could not have arisen if transnational corporations had already established themselves in the Brazilian market, that is (in our terms), if the level of foreign ownership and technological dominance had been high and the level of access by the *corpo técnico* was low. But fortunately the Brazilian government was able to take advantage of this "moment of transition" in international technology, before the foreign firms had developed an entrenched position in the market. This moment of transition provided the political opening – access – for Brazil's market reserve policy. That this absence of pressure from the TNCs is significant cannot be denied, as comparisons with experience of Asian NICs makes clear.[14] It is significant, as well, that in interviews with numerous key individuals in both the computer and pharmaceutical industries, virtually all interviewees emphasized the relative absence of computer TNCs in the Brazilian market at the time the market reserve was established as one of the key factors explaining the different outcomes in computers and pharmaceuticals.[15]

Nevertheless, as Evans himself admits, an explanation of the extended lifespan of the market reserve policy – long enough to allow at least some domestic firms to come into existence and to form joint ventures with foreign firms on profitable terms later on – requires more than this simple dependency argument. The moment of transition in computers – a period during which access was relatively high – may have facilitated the task of the *técnicos* in developing the government's policies for this sector. Yet (as Adler points out) the *técnicos*' desire and ability to persuade the military ministers to undertake the policies was crucial. Evans emphasizes, however, that the *técnicos* were able to do this mainly because the military leaders saw a clear connection between the computer industry and national security. Now that civilians are running the government, dependency could very well return. "As those who have been involved in the development of the Brazilian computer industry are acutely aware, victories such as those they have won are anything but permanent" (Evans 1986:804).

Despite the dangers Evans foresaw, his predictions did not entirely jibe with events. For it was the PMDB, the civilian (and far less national security-oriented) party that came to power after the transition to civilian rule in 1985, which enacted policies for the computer industry that went beyond what even the military (which had wanted to eliminate the policy as early as 1985) had wanted. Indeed, the industry's fiercest supporters all came from the ranks of the PMDB. And although the market reserve policy finally came to an end in 1992, it lasted long enough under civilian governments in Brazil – its last seven crucial years, from 1985 to 1992 – to enable Brazilian computer firms to acquire sufficient technological capabilities[16] to form joint ventures with foreign firms on terms more favorable than would otherwise have been possible. (Indeed, none of the domestic firms would even have existed to form joint ventures if it had not been for the market reserve policy.)

In order to explain how the market reserve policy lasted as long as it did, and to account for the whole problem of how shifts from military to democratic regimes – and political affinity – affect industrial policy in NICs, we must turn to the literature on authoritarianism and democratization. For the way in which domestic forces (e.g., the *corpos técnicos*) operate within the context of these different kinds of regimes can have a significant influence not only on what kinds of industries the government will *not* support – as many authors of the "strong domestic structure" vein suggest – but also, in some cases, on what industries it *will* support.

The literature on authoritarianism in Latin America has consisted of at least two kinds, corresponding broadly to two of the types described in Juan Linz's typology of authoritarian regimes (Linz 1975:175–411): bureaucratic-military authoritarian and organic statist (the latter of which I refer to here, in broad terms, as "corporatist"). Elements of both of these types can exist at the same time in the same regime: thus I refer to the military period in Brazil as the era of the "bureaucratic-authoritarian/corporatist" regime. But before moving on to applications, further elaboration of the concepts themselves is in order.

According to O'Donnell, who originally formulated the concept of bureaucratic-authoritarianism,[17] the way in which these regimes emerge governs which social groups they favor and which they exclude completely. One of the primary purposes of a bureaucratic-authoritarian (BA) regime is to move the economy toward a "deeper" phase of industrialization, i.e., one that involves moving from import-substitution industrialization and production of consumer goods to domestic manufacture of capital goods. The military and technocrats perceive that this goal is "threatened"[18] by excessive demands from the popular classes. In order to overcome the threat, the military establishes a regime which excludes the popular classes, encourages foreign investment, and promotes expansion of the capital goods sector. Thus, the social groups favored by the BA regime – those to whom O'Donnell refers as the "major social supports of the BA state" – are "the upper bourgeoisie and the 'modern' sectors of the middle class more closely tied to it" (O'Donnell 1979:297). Included also in the category of "social supports" of the regime are the representatives of "transnational and domestic finance capital," (O'Donnell 1979:297) as well as, of course, the military as institution.[19] In contrast, those social groups upon which BA regimes "inflict serious hardships" are "a good portion of the middle sector and the weakest (and more indisputably national) fractions of the bourgeoisie" (O'Donnell 1979:297). Labor unions and other representatives of the popular classes are demobilized, often by means of physical force.

A regime with these characteristics would not be inclined to support an industry, pharmaceuticals, on the basis of supporters' vague claims for the supposed – and at that only indirect and tenuous – "social" benefits the industry might provide. Given the military leaders' concerns, technocrats and ministers in charge of economic policymaking might be more amenable to arguments about the importance for *national security* of an indigenous pharmaceutical industry.[20] (After all, a nation dependent on the outside world for supplies of antibiotics, for example, might encounter serious difficulties in the case of a prolonged war if such supplies were cut off.) But such claims are, if anything, even more tenuous than the others. More reasonable to policymakers in this kind of regime would be the logic of supporting an arms-related sector with a much closer link to national security – the computer industry.[21] The question remains, however, as to the process by which such decisions are actually made.

Linz states that BA regimes "allow more or less pluralism" within sectors of society that represent the "social supports" of the state (Linz 1975:341). This characterization does not accurately reflect the reality of such regimes. For even if the interests of certain business groups, for example, might be more accommodated than those of, say, combative labor unions, the government does not respond directly, in a "government as cash register" kind of model, to the demands of even those groups. And contrary to O'Donnell's view, most labor unions and other associations, while demobilized, are not necessarily completely excluded as social actors; more often they continue to function but simply have little autonomy from state control. Hence, the system of interest representation that exists under such regimes is less similar to limited pluralism than it is to a more cooptative "state corporatism."[22]

Phillipe Schmitter, in *Interest Conflict and Political Change in Brazil*, shows how the Brazilian military government controlled and manipulated for its own purposes "associations" supposedly representing the interests of labor, national industry, and various other components of Brazilian society (Schmitter 1971). Schmitter describes this authoritarian state corporatism as a system in which top-level association leaders were well aware that if they became too assertive in opposing government policies the government would simply remove them from office. Thus even those groups that were favored by the government did not exert a forceful influence upon the government's policies; policy decisions flowed in strict hierarchical fashion from the top down rather than from the bottom up.

During the military years, this kind of decisionmaking was evident in both the computer and pharmaceutical industries. The activities of those lobbying for greater government support for these sectors were confined to a limited policymaking elite within the military regime, for technocrats and high-level officials from the various ministries made the most important decisions – in closed cabinet meetings – on these issues. The National Congress itself, while still in operation during most of the military era, had little influence on such matters until the closing years of the regime. Thus, the extent to which the policy elite, with their military and national security orientation, were already inclined toward support for certain sectors would naturally tend to affect their decisions more than any industry lobbying efforts.

The redemocratization literature which has arisen in response to recent transitions to democratic rule in Latin America has continued to emphasize the enduring elements of this elitist, "top-down" tradition. The theme that runs throughout most of this literature is that transitions to democracy have come about not as a result of social actors pressuring the government for change (although such factors may have affected the timing of the transitions), but rather as a result of a process of bargaining among elites within the government (O'Donnell, Schmitter, Whitehead 1986; Stepan 1988; Baloyra 1987; Selcher 1986; Levine 1988:376–94, Mainwaring, O'Donnell,Valenzuela 1992). Thus, common terms used in much of this literature are "democratization from above," *conciliação pelo alto* (conciliation from above), and "transition through transaction."

Although this literature is correct in emphasizing the importance of continuity in these regimes, particularly with regard to the military's enduring presence, it tends to limit itself to analysis of the political maneuvering involved in bringing transitions about, rather than to study of how the new regimes actually operate once installed. Given that a great deal of the literature was written before much could be said about the new democracies, this particular emphasis was inevitable. Nevertheless, even when some preliminary efforts are made to assess the new regimes themselves (e.g., O'Donnell and Schmitter's *Tentative Conclusions About New Democracies*, Vol. 4 in the *Transitions From Authoritarian Rule* collection (1986) or Mainwaring, O'Donnell, Valenzuela (1992) the analysis points to a continuation of elitist, undemocratic forms of policymaking.

This view is generally valid. But, as we have argued here, where high-tech industrial policy is concerned – contrary to what one would expect – there are some important exceptions. In fact, under democratic, civilian rule, members of those *corpos técnicos* affiliated with *particular kinds* of high-tech industries, far from keeping policy decisions out of the public realm, can make use of their political affinity with civilian, democratically elected politicians (and large segments of public opinion) to completely alter a nation's industrial policy. In attempting to explain why some sectors receive high levels of government political support and others do not, my study makes this factor the central aspect of the analysis.

PRELIMINARY SURVEY OF CASE OUTCOMES

Because this book focuses on political outcomes, we need to make a preliminary assessment here of how and to what extent the levels of government political support differed for the two respective industries.[23] Particularly important is how the change in political regime – the shift from military to civilian rule – affected the government's policies toward the two industries.

Because the shift in regime is of special importance, the time-frame to be used in this book is from approximately 1980 (latter part of the military regime) to the mid-1990s. Hence, the emphasis here is not on how initial policies arose but on the extent to which lobbyists for an industry were able to maintain support for their policy agenda over time.[24]

In the late 1970s, the military government took very different actions toward government agencies charged with promoting the interests of the computer and pharmaceutical industries. In 1979 the government shifted authority over the market reserve policy from CAPRE (Commission for the Coordination of Electronic Data Processing Activities) to the new Special Secretariat on Informatics (SEI), under the direct authority of the National Security Council, and, therefore, the president. The newly created SEI had broad powers to decide which computer products would be protected under the market reserve, what kinds of direct investment projects foreign firms could undertake, and how government subsidies and incentives for indigenous research efforts would be allocated. After 1984, with the market reserve policy under severe pressure from transnational corporations (TNCs) such as IBM, the Brazilian Congress voted to increase SEI's powers even further.

The government's treatment of the *Central de Medicamentos* (CEME), shows how its policy toward the pharmaceutical industry differed from its stance toward the computer sector. Created in 1971 to serve as both a state-owned pharmaceutical firm and a distributor of medications to the poor, CEME initially had broad, far-ranging goals. These included manufacturing medications at low cost and the funding of indigenous research efforts in the pharmaceutical industry. In 1975, however, the government greatly weakened CEME's abilities to promote indigenous development in the industry by removing it from the direct control of the president and dividing responsibility for its activities among five different ministries. Under the new arrangement, the handing out of medications to the poor took priority; actual production was placed much lower on CEME's agenda. This action showed the government's reluctance to permit CEME to have authority in pharmaceuticals similar in any way to that of SEI in computers.

The gradual shift toward civilian rule, and the eventual rise to power (first in the National Congress and later in the Executive Branch as well) of the opposition, left-of-center *Partido do Movimento Democrático Brasileiro* (PMDB) party, would seem to have created the conditions for a shift in the government's levels of political support for the two industries. After all, the PMDB's official slogan (already mentioned) was "everything for the social welfare." One might suspect, then, that support for the national security-related computer industry would decline, while support for the social-related (or at least, not military-related) pharmaceutical industry would increase. Still another reason for the new government to diminish support for the computer industry, as we have already pointed out, was that just as the democratic transition was reaching its peak in the mid-1980s, the rising civilian political leaders were increasingly having to face the issue of negotiating repayment of Brazil's enormous foreign debt. To annoy foreign governments, and in particular the United States, with protectionist policies in the computer industry at that time would not seem to be very sensible.

Nevertheless, government political support for the computer industry *increased*, if anything, and after a brief rise, support for the pharmaceutical industry remained at low levels. The outcomes of attempts by supporters of the two industries to present legislation in the National Congress, of international negotiations with developed nations, of the National Congress' deliberations over policy during the presidential campaign of 1989, and of policies under the Collor Administration support this assessment.

In the early 1980s proponents of a *Lei de Informática*, a law which would institutionalize the market reserve policy, began to carry out a strategy to persuade the National Congress to support their agenda. They soon gained the trust of many members of the National Congress, often serving as technical advisers to key politicians (such as members of the Science and Technology Commission). Combining these strategic posts with a massive, thorough lobbying effort designed to sway the general public as well as the *parlementares*,[25] the proponents succeeded, when the time came to vote on the *Lei* in 1984, in winning an overwhelmingly favorable outcome. Ironically, this success for what the military had always seen as a policy crucial to the interests of "national security" came about just as the military regime was coming to an end, and the military government itself was decreasing its support for the policy. Indeed, the strongest support of all came from democratic-minded politicians who distrusted the military.

Advocates of similar legislation for the pharmaceutical industry suffered a different fate. When the GIFAR, or Interministerial Group for the Pharmaceutical Industry (composed of representatives of CEME and the Industrial Development Council), proposed – in 1982, at the close of the military years – a national program for the sector that also incorporated elements of a market reserve, it faced great opposition within the government itself. After three years of stalling, and after the ministers opposed to the program had made many alterations, the government finally implemented the program in 1984, the same year the *Lei de Informática* was enacted. However, in the GIFAR program's final form the original "market reserve" provisions were so weakened that they did little to block imports, they permitted joint ventures, and they provided benefits to the sector as a whole, foreign and national firms alike, which had originally been intended for national firms alone. Even after the more socially-minded PMDB came to power and some of the pharmaceutical industry's supporters in the National Congress proposed legislation (in 1985 and 1986) to enact policies similar to the original GIFAR program, President Sarney vetoed it, citing the bad timing of such legislation as Brazil prepared to discuss the computer market reserve with the US. This outcome, and lack of further attempts to propose such legislation, demonstrate the continuing low level of government support for the pharmaceutical sector, despite political factors that should have favored it.

In the international arena, the outcome of negotiations with the United States in 1986 on the computer market reserve are another instance of the civilian government's strong political support for the computer sector. On four separate occasions that year the Brazilian and United States governments met to resolve their contentions over the market reserve policy. Despite strong pressures on the part of the US government for the Brazilians to abandon this policy, and what would seem to be a strong interest on Brazil's part to not antagonize one of its major creditors, the Brazilian negotiating teams held firm. They were backed in this position by the staunch commitment of the ruling PMDB party to maintain the market reserve regardless of US threats and diplomatic efforts.

In this area, too, the pharmaceutical industry fared poorly in comparison with the computer sector. As mentioned earlier, Sarney vetoed legislation for a pharmaceutical market reserve for fear of jeopardizing relations with the US at a crucial time. And even before this, the source of the divisions within the government over the original GIFAR proposal had stemmed from international pressures. When the transnational corporations in the pharmaceutical industry had heard of the GIFAR program, they had immediately demanded that representatives of the British, American, and German commerce associations send telexes to all the ministers who would be involved in it, including then-President Figuereido, saying that if it were instituted in its proposed form their governments would make Brazil's upcoming debt negotiations very difficult. In both this instance and the later case, the government's level of political support for the sector was insufficient to overcome such international pressures.

The outcomes of the 1989 debates in the National Congress over the two industries showed still further the tendency for differences in levels of government political support for the computer and pharmaceutical industries. In the computer sector, key members of the Science and Technology Committee in the Chamber of Deputies (e.g., the President and Vice-President of the committee, and the *relator*, the *deputado*, or congressman, who writes the committee's final report), as well as key members of the equivalent body in the Senate, remained strongly in favor of fairly strict market reserve provisions in the *Planin II*, the government's second three-year plan for the industry. Most opposition within the Science and Technology Committee did *not* arise from those with a principled stand against state intervention, poor economic performance under current arrangements, etc. Rather, it came from those committee members with links to large telecommunications firms, who opposed SEI's regulations on foreign telecommunications technology imports. Because opponents such as these could not easily defend their stance as being in the best interests of the nation as a whole, their views were not very persuasive to other politicians. Hence, the computer sector's agenda continued to prevail.

In the pharmaceutical sector, the main arena for debate in the National Congress after 1988 was the Senate Investigating Commission on the Pharmaceutical Industry. While one of the main purposes of this Commission was to investigate the problem of foreign domination in the industry, the Commission itself met rarely and came to few conclusions of any substance. That this Commission would propose any measures of substance to correct the most severe problems with the industry seemed highly unlikely. Most observers, including one knowledgeable and important member of the Commission itself, judged it to be a complete failure.[26] Thus, in contrast once again with the computer industry, government political support for pharmaceuticals was low by this measure, too.

Finally, after the Collor Administration took office in April, 1990, the trend continued. Despite President Collor's firm commitment to liberalize the Brazilian economy, he was able initially only to bring about a gradual – and even then only partial – phasing out of the computer market reserve.[27] In the pharmaceutical sector, on the other hand, all potential proposals for any sort of market reserve were quickly eliminated from political discourse. Not only that, but the one relatively narrow goal that those in the pharmaceutical sector had managed to articulate and lobby for with some fervor, the non-recognition of patents on pharmaceutical products, was almost immediately overturned.

Clearly, then, for the years analyzed here, policy outcomes in these two industries have been markedly different. Such differences make these two cases useful theoretically to demonstrate how a strong "political affinity" between a particular high-tech industry's *corpo técnico*, and the dominant political party or coalition can affect industrial policies in NICs undergoing democratization.

PREVIEW

The chapters that follow develop this argument more fully and provide evidence to support it. Chapters 2 and 3 both examine the dependent variable, outcomes of the *corpos técnicos'* lobbying efforts during first the military and then the civilian eras. Chapter 2 discusses the computer *corpo técnico's* strategy and outcomes; Chapter 3, the strategy and outcomes of the pharmaceutical *corpo técnico*. Chapter 4 examines the political characteristics of the two *corpos técnicos*, demonstrating (by means of survey data and interviews) that members of the computer *corpo técnico* had a more leftist, activist political orientation in comparison with members of the pharmaceutical *corpo técnico*. Chapter 5 discusses the other variables in the overall model, and takes a preliminary look at economic outcomes in the two industries. Chapter 6 surveys the secondary literature to apply the argument to the nuclear industry in Brazil, Argentina, and South Korea. Finally, the concluding chapter discusses the broader implications of the book's findings for the literature on democratization and development, and for the making of industrial policy in the NICs.

2   The computer industry

No less remarkable than the development of a domestic computer industry in Brazil was the enormous political support the industry had and maintained through successive political regimes. The purpose of this chapter is to describe and delineate the extent of that support during both the military and civilian regimes, discussing, in the process, the role of the computer *corpo técnico* in promoting it. In order to do this, we will first examine how political support for the computer industry evolved during the military era, and then how the special characteristics of the computer *corpo técnico* enabled it actually to increase political support for the industry during the transition to democratic rule. Finally, we will show that the *corpo técnico* was also able to maintain support for the industry, relative to some other sectors, after the arrival of the Collor Administration.

In the succeeding chapter, on the pharmaceutical industry, we will discuss in some detail the distinct role of each segment of the *corpo técnico*: the *técnicos*, *empresários*, and university professors.[1] In the pharmaceutical sector, different elements of the *corpo técnico* really did have different stances and approaches with regard to the promotion of government political support for the sector. In that case, therefore, separate discussion of each branch of the *corpo técnico* seems warranted. In the computer industry, on the other hand, members of the *corpo técnico* (most with highly advanced graduate training) were able easily to shift back and forth from being university professors, *técnicos*, and *empresários*. Many were members of each of these branches of the *corpo técnico* at different stages of their careers. Partly for this reason, different segments of the computer *corpo técnico* did not have significant disagreements about policy. In this chapter, then, we will *not* emphasize the separateness and distinctness of each of the branches of the *corpo técnico*, but will focus on the actions of the similarly motivated individuals in the computer *corpo técnico* as a whole.

THE MILITARY ERA

Successive military governments took the necessary steps to get the computer industry started, and they continued to support the industry until nearly the end of the military's reign. (As noted in Chapter 1, the relatively high degree of access facilitated the military and later the civilian government's efforts in this regard.) The military goverment supported the computer industry so strongly because it believed that doing so would serve not only the military itself as an institution, but Brazil's national security concerns (broadly defined) as well.

The computer *corpo técnico* was less important during the military years than it would become later, because at this time, like the computer industry itself, it was only in its incipient stages. While electronics engineers and professors existed in the tens of thousands in Brazil, the crucial business component of the *corpo técnico* was only gradually coming into existence, and did not really attain significant numbers until the closing years of the military regime.

As mentioned in the introductory chapter, Adler argues that "ideological guerillas" infiltrated the government to get the military ministers to support the computer industry. But more important than this "infiltration" was the fact that important elements of the military *already* supported development of the industry, as has been documented widely (Helena 1980:73–109; Evans 1986:791–808; Dantas 1988). Further elaboration of this assertion illustrates how policymaking under the military regime differed significantly from that under civilian rule.

From the beginning, Brazil's computer program depended on political support from high-ranking military officials within the government. Officials from the *Banco Nacional de Desenvolvimento Económico* (BNDE), Brazil's government development bank, had been considering funding a computer project in the country for some time when, in 1968, they were approached by Navy officials with a similar idea. Because the Navy had recently purchased some high-tech Italian frigates, and was concerned about insufficient national capability to maintain and repair these vessels in the event of war, Navy officials saw that development of some indigenous technological capacity in computers was crucial. In this way, development of a domestic computer industry in Brazil became tightly linked, in the minds of key military officials, with national security.

Others have commented on the unlikely pairing of the vaguely leftist intellectual engineers and scientists,[2] the ones who had the technical capabilities in computers and who were at the forefront of efforts to establish a domestic computer industry in Brazil, with the *militares*, the conservative, no-nonsense military officials who sought to develop a computer industry for somewhat different reasons (Dantas 1988). And indeed, these two groups were naturally somewhat antagonistic toward each other. At the very least, as Chapter 4 attempts to demonstrate, they were not inclined to share the same political viewpoints. Nevertheless, united by their common goal, they were able to forge a mutually beneficial if somewhat awkward and unnatural working relationship.

A significant factor contributing to the ability of these two disparate groups to get along together was that the military officials who were involved in efforts to establish a computer industry tended to be somewhat different from other Brazilian military officials, and far different, certainly, from the common perception of Brazilian military officers as a whole. First of all, the military officials involved with the program came from the Navy, as already explained above, and also from the Air Force. Because these two branches of the Armed Forces had relatively higher standards for recruitment and their particular institutional styles were highly professional, they were composed of relatively well-educated personnel. This in itself worked to bridge the gap between the two groups; also important, however, and concomitant with the higher levels of education, were these branches' less reactionary views on such matters as democratic government.[3]

The key pair of individuals who made up the Special Working Group (GTE), formed by the military government in 1971 – a collaborative effort of the *Banco Nacional de Desenvolvimento Ecónomico* and the Ministry of the Navy – illustrate this point. Ricardo Saur, the BNDE's representative in the GTE, had reasons for wanting to develop a domestic computer industry that he shared with many other computer *corpo técnico* members. Having done postgraduate work in computer science at Stanford, Saur was still young and eager to make a contribution beyond working as a salesman for IBM, which was perhaps the most relevant opportunity that Brazil could offer someone with his specific qualifications if it did *not* develop such an industry. Thus, he accepted the offer, when it came in the form of an invitation from the Director of the Science and Technology section of the BNDE, to work toward this goal – even if, as Dantas (1988) noted, working with a military man might potentially have seemed an awkward prospect.[4]

Frigate Captain José Luis dos Guaranys Rego, the Navy's representative to the GTE, was a different sort of man than Saur, with different motivations. He was first and foremost a military man, with concerns that could only be foreign to frustrated engineers, returning from their graduate programs and looking for some significant and fulfilling niche in the authoritarian Brazil to which they were returning. Nevertheless, Guaranys was a highly educated and technically trained man himself, having received a Ph.D. in electrical engineering from Syracuse University many years before. This fact, and the broadened outlook that came with such a background, eased Guaranys's working relationship with his civilian counterpart; it allowed the two men to argue over technical points as colleagues engaged in a common endeavor. But significant differences in outlook remained.[5]

While better-educated *militares* in the Air Force or Navy, such as Guaranys, may have had easier relations with the *corpo técnico* – or at least what existed of it at the time – than officials in the Army could ever have had, the relationship was never one with which the *corpo técnico* and *militares* as a whole could pursue with wholehearted enthusiasm and harmony. Key members of the *corpo técnico*, indeed the most prominent and elite of their number, chafed under the circumstances of this uneasy alliance. The electrical engineer (and later *empresário*) Edson Fregni, at the forefront of developing the new technology in Brazil, as well as in shaping the political agenda and program that would get the industry established, was a case in point. He frequently took the opportunity to make his own political views – which differed considerably from those of the military officials with whom he had to work – known in a way that was sure to make the *militares* uncomfortable.

For instance, at a São Paulo industry-wide meeting in 1983 to receive the award for Brazil's Engineer of the Year – for having done the most to advance the cause of his profession – Fregni gave a speech to the assembled officials, including prominent members of the military establishment, that seemed designed to upset officialdom. In the speech he stressed that "[i]t is useless to seek technological development... without democratic processes to guarantee that we undertake this development with the goal of meeting the basic needs of our people" (Dantas 1988:256). And, at the conclusion, much to the consternation of the military authorities present, Fregni shouted the slogan: "Direct Elections for President of the Republic!" (Dantas 1988:256).

As founder of the *Movimento Brasil de Informática* (MBI), to be discussed at greater length in the next section, Fregni (and other members of the *corpo técnico*) had still another means to express such views. The MBI did not really become important until the time of the debate over the *Lei de Informática*, at the close of the military years, but even somewhat earlier it had (under Fregni's guidance) established a clear political agenda in favor of such issues as democracy and the plight of the Brazilian Indians. In an act that, according to Fregni himself, "got us into a bit of trouble and brought a lot of complaints from the *militares* involved in the [computer] program,"[6] Fregni sent out one of the MBI's reports with two diagonal yellow stripes, the emblem of the *Diretas Já!* (direct presidential elections now!) movement of 1983–4, on the cover. This occurred at a time when the *Diretas Já!* campaign represented strong opposition to the military government and to the entire authoritarian regime upon which it was based. To express support for the movement was a risky thing to do.

Such actions on the part of Edson Fregni and other *corpo técnico* members not only demonstrated their unease with the military regime, but also seemed to indicate the tendency of relatively young people of that particular era in Brazil – which, in comparison with their counterparts in the pharmaceutical sector, the computer *corpo técnico* members were – to take risks, to question authority, and to taunt officials representing the "Establishment."[7] A comment by Senator Roberto Campos, a prominent (and elderly) member of the then ruling PDS military party, highlights this point. Senator Campos, a strong opponent of the market reserve policy, referred to Fregni as "that foolish adolescent." Fregni, in particular, but other members of the computer *corpo técnico* as well, did have the aforementioned qualities of this generation of youth about them. Even glancing at photographs of the most active *corpo técnico* members of the day – i.e., the 1970s – reveals their penchant for the style of young people at that time: long hair, beards, an informal manner of dress. It is significant to note that politically conservative young people of that time did not dress like this!

Thus, the attitudes and political orientation of the computer *corpo técnico* certainly did not facilitate its ability to work with the military patrons of Brazil's computer program. That the two groups collaborated at all is what surprises most commentators; that the alliance held together as long as it did is even more surprising. But the built-in tensions and conflicts of interest were bound to come to the fore as time wore on. Over time the military's strong enthusiasm for strict adherence to the market reserve policy waned. The policy was no longer serving the military's interests, for Brazil's computer industry was simply not able to supply all of the military's needs for the very latest in technology at prices competitive on the world market.

This might have presented a dilemma for the computer *corpo técnico*, which had no special influence over the military government to affect policy. (Indeed, if the "infiltration" of the "ideological guerillas" was as great as some would have us believe,[8] then the government's shift of course, or at least its declining enthusiasm for the computer program, would be difficult to understand.) But the computer *corpo técnico* members were fortunate in that the political orientation of the government was changing in a way that would suit their particular political characteristics. Moreover, they were astute enough to take advantage of this situation, and use it to win increased political support for a computer program that, until then, had appeared to be on the decline.

DEMOCRATIC TRANSITION AND BEYOND

The transition to democracy in Brazil presented new opportunities to the computer *corpo técnico*. A long, gradual process, the *abertura*, or opening up of the political regime, had its beginnings in the early 1980s. The military had planned to return Brazil to democratic rule all along when the time was right; as the 1980s wore on, however, events accelerated and the process began to take on a life of its own. These changes brought new politicians, members of the opposition Brazilian Democratic Movement Party (PMDB), to positions of authority. As Chapter 4 will demonstrate, these new politicians had much in common politically with members of the computer *corpo técnico*. *Corpo técnico* members were able to take advantage of this situation to increase political support for the computer industry even as the democratic transition was taking place.

That the new democratic politicians would support the computer *corpo técnico*'s political agenda went against all the odds. In the first place, the military government was itself eventually to pull back, for sound economic reasons, from that policy the computer *corpo técnico* most vehemently supported, the market reserve. The rigid import restrictions the computer *corpo técnico* advocated prevented other sectors within the Brazilian economy from obtaining access to cheaper, high-quality computers on the international market. Moreover, the computer industry was strongly associated in the PMDB politicians' minds with the military regime. Indeed, important PMDB politician (and after 1982 congressional elections, member of the *Câmara dos Deputados*[9]) Cristina Tavares, one of the strongest opponents of that regime, had given a powerful speech before the *Câmara* calling for the dismantling of the *Secretaria Especial de Informática*. Thus, for the computer *corpo técnico* to expect continued high levels of support for their programs, much less increased support, seemed foolish.

Yet increased political support for the industry was precisely what the greater political affinity between the rising PMDB politicians and the computer *corpo técnico* brought about. Ironically enough, Cristina Tavares herself was at the forefront of the political struggle that resulted in this increased support. The remainder of this chapter seeks to describe the extent of this increased support, and to show how it came about.

By the early 1980s, when the PMDB was becoming sufficiently important politically to warrant such attention, the computer *corpo técnico* had developed into a significant (or at least potentially significant) force. Technically trained personnel working within the industry had grown from a few frustrated engineers to individuals numbering in the tens of thousands. Moreover, by the 1980s the *corpo técnico* had come to consist of more than just engineers, scientists, and professors. As the computer industry grew and became profitable, the business people working within the sector, too, developed a strong interest in maintaining government support for it. This part of the *corpo técnico*, with significant financial resources and talent at its command, was crucial to the computer *corpo técnico*'s successes (as this chapter will contend throughout).

The event that galvanized the computer *corpo técnico* into action was changes in government policy on protective tariffs for personal computers. The *corpo técnico* realized that, given increasing political liberalization, and later, the highly successful showing for opposition parties in the 1982 elections for members of Congress and state governors (the first since the military coup of 1964), collaboration with the military was soon to outlive its usefulness. The new democrats in Brazil, if naturally antagonistic toward the computer industry, would have to be approached and their political consciousness about the importance of the industry raised. Of course, the protectionist market reserve policy was becoming less "rational" – from a purely technocratic standpoint of economic efficiency – all the time. But the similarity of political views between the computer *corpo técnico* members and the PMDB politicians would make the task of convincing the politicians far less difficult.

The *corpo técnico* began to carry out these plans even before the 1980s. In 1978, the Association of Professional Data Processors (APPD) met with two federal deputies, Marcelo Cerqueira and Modesto da Silveira, both members of the PMDB, and persuaded them to commit themselves to bringing the *informática*[10] issue up for debate in the National Congress. These two deputies, known for their outspokenness in defense of political prisoners during the harshest years of the military dictatorship, were appropriate choices in the APPD's effort to force the government to discuss the issue openly in the National Congress. Their political credentials as courageous challengers of the *status quo* and their membership in the PMDB were significant.[11] The APPD also made the issue a focus of concern at the annual conference of the Society of Informatics Users (SUCESU) in the same year, and sponsored a meeting about the subject which many related organizations, and some federal politicians, attended.

Such activities made the PMDB take notice of *informática* as a national issue meriting further study.[12] This was clear when the leader of the PMDB in the Chamber of Deputies created the PMDB's Informatics Commission, and put another *deputado*, Mauricio Fruet, in charge of it.

Fruet knew virtually nothing about informatics but now suddenly found himself in charge of coordinating the activities of an entire commission dealing with the subject. He needed technical advice and called on a young, articulate electrical engineer, Milton Seligman, to assist him.[13] Seligman, also a member of the PMDB, had strong views about the importance of Brazil's developing its own technology in *informática*. At the same time, he was ideologically left of center and a strong supporter of the movement for democracy in Brazil.[14] With these political inclinations, common among members of the computer *corpo técnico*, Seligman quickly won the trust of Mauricio Fruet and other key members of the PMDB.[15] Thus, when he (along with a colleague in the *Secretaria Especial de Informática*) produced a document for the PMDB's informatics commission on the social, political and economic importance of informatics, his arguments carried special weight.[16] Indeed, Mauricio Fruet helped begin the process of turning Seligman's key proposal – that the National Informatics Policy (PNI) should no longer be carried out by government decree but should be institutionalized, democratically, as law in the National Congress – into one of the PMDB's political objectives.

Seligman also played a key role as adviser to the *deputada* Cristina Tavares, an outspoken representative of the left wing of the PMDB. As mentioned above, Tavares, a strong opponent of the military regime, was highly critical of the government's creation of the *Secretaria Especial de Informática* (SEI), formed in 1979 to coordinate the national informatics program. Specifically, SEI coordinated the policies limiting imports on small computers. Because SEI was the brainchild of the military technocrats, and was headed by former military officers, Tavares lambasted it as a step toward the strengthening of the military regime (Tavares 1979). She went so far as to present a bill in the Chamber of Deputies that would ensure citizens' access to personal information stored in government data banks. Having read Seligman's report for the PMDB Informatica Commission, Tavares called on Seligman to serve as her technical adviser in writing up this bill. It was from working with Seligman that Tavares began to take a broader view of the informatics issue, and to realize the importance of computer technology to Brazil's economic development.[17]

It was highly significant that Tavares and Seligman had very similar political views;[18] this facilitated the extent to which Seligman, who had great respect for the *deputada*, could began to increase her awareness about some of the larger issues involved with informatics. As one *corpo técnico* member involved with lobbying politicians said in an interview, "the creation of SEI created an opening for us to start talking about broader issues."[19] Soon Cristina Tavares, who had previously viewed SEI with great suspicion, became one of the staunchest defenders of SEI's overall goal: to limit imports of small computers from abroad to permit expansion of local industry. *Deputada* Tavares was to play a key role in the *corpo técnico*'s struggles to obtain its objectives in the years ahead.[20]

The most important of those struggles was that leading up to the 1984 *Lei de Informática* (Informatics Law), which institutionalized the *Política Nacional de Informática* (PNI), or National Informatics Policy. As mentioned, Milton Seligman and other leading members of the *corpo técnico*[21] saw that the growing importance of the National Congress provided them with an opportunity to legitimize the PNI by having the National Congress decide on it democratically (Dantas 1988:255–90; Fregni 1985:213–34). That done, the policy – especially its most controversial component, the market reserve – would be better able to withstand pressures both from opponents within Brazil as well as from the United States. As one surprising source put it (surprising since he was the General Secretary of the Brazilian National Security Council – not the usual position for someone concerned with democratic niceties – and a military general to boot): "[t]he Americans are very persistent in pursuing their objectives, but at the same time they are very formal and observe the law at all costs. If we have [the market reserve institutionalized as] a law they will think twice before putting on the pressure."[22]

Yet while the *corpo técnico* leaders sensed opportunities, there were also great difficulties to surmount. Namely, the *corpo técnico* had to convince members of what since 1982 had become a more democracy-oriented (and specifically, PMDB-oriented) Congress to support a program founded under the auspices of the military dictatorship – and clearly of special interest to the military. Some of this work had begun earlier; for example, Milton Seligman's efforts had paid off well in winning Cristina Tavares over into taking a friendly position toward the national industry. But putting the PNI into place by democratic means, while having potentially broader consequences, was at the same time much more complicated than lobbying one *deputada*. Not willing to lose the opportunity, and having themselves strong sympathies with the democratization movement,[23] the computer *corpo técnico* members swung into action.

The informal leader of the *corpo técnico's* lobbying campaign for approval of its version of the policy was the *empresário* Edson Fregni, whose importance has already merited extended discussion. As mentioned, Fregni, a strong opponent of the military regime, was inspired by the mid-1980s *Diretas Já!* campaign to create his own movement, the *Movimento Brasil de Informática* (MBI).[24] The purpose of the MBI was to coordinate the lobbying efforts of a variety of groups which sought to maintain the market reserve. The MBI arose because of a particular set of circumstances: increasing pressure from the United States to overturn the market reserve, and the upcoming debate within the National Congress over not only the market reserve but the National Informatics Plan as a whole.

As Fregni saw it, the MBI was a way not only to coordinate the computer *corpo técnico's* efforts but also to deflect criticism that those fighting for the market reserve were only those businessmen who would benefit from its continued existence.[25] Local *empresários* in the industry who sought to maintain the market reserve were in fact the most prominent and active group within the MBI. Indeed, they already had their own highly capable organization, Abicomp (Brazilian Association of Computers and Peripherals), which listed, among others, Edson Fregni himself as one of its past presidents.

Other organizations were included under the MBI's broad umbrella: the Association of Professional Data Processors (APPD), the Society of Informatics Users (SUCESU), and even (reflecting Fregni's particular political concerns) Indian rights groups. Yet these organizations were less important than Abicomp in the overall lobbying campaign, and continue to be less important today.[26] The MBI's 1984 lobbying campaign itself was perhaps the zenith of the computer *corpo técnico*'s effectiveness. Much of the effort focused on increasing the public's awareness about the importance of an indigenous computer industry. The goal was to persuade the *parlamentares*[27] to vote in favor of the strong market reserve and other provisions in the *corpo técnico*'s version of the bill.[28] To get attention for the cause, Edson Fregni even organized an MBI march down the streets of São Paulo. People carried signs with slogans such as "the technology is ours," a reference to the nationalist campaigns of the past for national ownership of Brazilian oil fields, which had proclaimed "the oil is ours."[29] But perhaps even stronger than the nationalist symbolism was the strong resemblance of this little march to the *Diretas Já!* (Direct Elections Now!) demonstrations going on simultaneously, on a much larger scale, throughout Brazil. The intent of the MBI's leaders to link the MBI with the fight for democracy was clear.

Of greater practical consequence than this small demonstration, however, was the computer *corpo técnico*'s verbal battles with its opponents – a loose alliance of computer users and proponents of free trade – in the National Congress and on the pages of the Brazilian press. Lacking the persuasive political arguments the computer *corpo técnico* was using, the users/freetraders resorted to somewhat technical and pedantic – although, as later results would suggest, perhaps fairly accurate – explanations of how a restrictive import policy would impede growth in all sectors, of how protectionism inevitably lead to inefficiency, etc. One particularly harsh opponent was Senator Roberto Campos, former Minister of Planning, who lambasted the market reserve as completely unsound and referred to Edson Fregni's arguments as "naive" and "infantile" (Dantas 1988:277).

The *corpo técnico*'s arguments, on the other hand – in favor of a more restrictive import policy for computers, with substantial government intervention in the form of subsidies, etc. – were couched in terms that would link such a policy to the PMDB's democratic stance. The link was not immediately obvious. Yet the *corpo técnico*'s argument, which came to be picked up by prominent PMDB politicians, was that passage of the proposed National Informatics Plan (PNI), would represent an expansion of the National Congress's powers over the executive.[30] After some twenty years of authoritarian rule, during which a technocratic elite arbitrarily had made decisions on such matters by executive decree, the National Congress would now attempt to initiate and approve its own version of a controversial and important industrial policy. Furthermore, under the terms of the legislation the National Congress would evaluate it and decide whether to approve it again every three years.

A lobbying strategy that placed the proposed legislation in the context of the fight for democracy and expanding the power of the National Congress seemed likely to be effective, for these were themes that were foremost on the minds of the PMDB *parlamentares* during the latter part of 1983 and 1984. That important politicians in the PMDB embraced the *corpo técnico*'s view of the PNI wholeheartedly was evident from the testimony of the PMDB's presidential candidate in 1984, Tancredo Neves, before the congressional commission studying the issue. Neves made clear that the time had come for important national decisions, and specifically the government's policy toward the computer industry, to be made democratically. Not doing so would only create more problems for the country. Making reference to the PMDB's concerns about social welfare and democracy, Neves argued that:

> [i]n many countries – among them our own – there arose the tendency to turn over to the technocrats the solution of the problem represented by the allocation of resources. The result of this mistake was, invariably, the concentration of income, the increase in regional inequalities, financial speculation and intolerable concessions to national sovereignty... only with democracy can we develop an authentic national [informatics] program.
>
> (Neves 1984:20)

Deputado Ulysses Guimarães, leader of the PMDB in the Chamber of Deputies, described his similar views in support of the PNI soon after it had been voted into law:

> For the first time, after long years of dictatorship by the technocrats, the National Congress discussed and established a Technological and Industrial Policy of vital importance to the future of Brazil. As a result of this debate not only was our national sovereignty guaranteed, but also democratic mechanisms for the administration of this policy were created. The National Congress maintains control over the fundamental decisions for the sector, by means of approval of the PNI, reviewed every three years. Every three years, therefore, the Legislature will debate, with Brazilian society, the course and priorities for informatics. These are the methods of democracy.
>
> (Guimarães 1985:13)

It is somewhat ironic that these politicians spoke of overcoming "dictatorship by the technocrats" when, in a sense, that dictatorship would continue.

While under more "democratic" forms of decisionmaking technocrats might no longer make the decisions and impose their will from above, the technically trained members of the *corpo técnico* would continue to exert significant influence over the politicians, who lacked that expertise. An informal survey by *Veja* magazine at the time the PNI was being discussed showed that members of the National Congress knew almost nothing about some of the most basic aspects of the policy. One *deputado* estimated that "less than 4 percent of the members of the National Congress [had] a broad view of the national informatics program" ("Confusão..." 1986:97). Reliance on members of the *corpo técnico*, with both the proper technical and – in the case of such advisers as Milton Seligman, Fernando Calicchio, Edson Fregni, etc. – the proper political credentials, would certainly tend to make the *parlamentares* more open to the *corpo técnico*'s arguments. Thus, the politicians would be inclined to accept the view that voting for the PNI was perfectly consistent with supporting the democratization process, that, indeed, it was what those who favored democracy should do. It was not too surprising, then, that when the time came for the vote on the PNI in the National Congress, it passed easily.

At this point, a certain caveat is in order. From the data provided thus far one might conclude that civilian *corpo técnico* members, with their democratic political inclinations, were the only ones pushing for the passage of the strong version of the PNI. Certainly, the new policy was more restrictive than what the official military-related party, the PDS – with traditionally a more economically liberal orientation than the PMDB – was willing to support. Nevertheless, there were important exceptions to the liberal economic position within the PDS party as well as among the military *técnicos* who were in charge of Brazil's computer program. For example, Colonel Edson Dytz and Colonel José Ezil Veiga da Rocha, both in charge of SEI at different times during the military regime, were two of the market reserve's strongest proponents. One point to remember when considering such exceptions is that, as with Frigate Captain Guaranys in the beginning of the computer industry in Brazil, these two individuals were highly trained *técnicos* from the Air Force, the branch of the military that traditionally represented the best-educated personnel, with views different from the majority of the military. More important, however, was that the politically liberal civilians, such as Milton Seligman, Edson Fregni, etc., were providing the driving force behind the lobbying of the *parlamentares*.

THE NEW REPUBLIC: THE EARLY YEARS

The computer *corpo técnico*'s ability to make use of its political affinity with the PMDB politicians continued after the transition to the democratic New

Republic government in 1985. The computer *corpo técnico*'s influence over the ruling PMDB became even more clearly evident in 1986, when the Sarney Administration experienced strong international pressure to overturn the computer market reserve, yet refused to give in.

Rising conflicts with the United States over the computer market reserve meant that the government would have to meet with US negotiating teams to iron out these conflicts. Four such meetings took place in 1986 in three cities: Brussels, Mexico City, and Paris. In each instance, the United States pressured the Brazilian government to withdraw or at least modify its computer market reserve. And in each case, the Brazilian government refused. Essentially, it gave no ground whatsoever at these meetings; the government considered them more as information sessions for the US negotiators, to explain why Brazil would not concede ("Controversia..." 1986). (One of the main reasons the government supplied was that the market reserve, as a law passed by the National Congress, could not simply be altered through international negotiation. Changes would require another act of the National Congress. Thus, as General Venturini had foreseen years earlier, the Brazilians were able to make use – in their efforts to impress the Americans of the legitimacy of their actions – of the legitimacy that a democratically instituted law conferred on the market reserve policy.)

The negotiators from the Itamaraty (Brazil's Foreign Office) held firm on the market reserve policy because it had the wholehearted support from top politicians, including President Sarney[31] and the later President of the Chamber of Deputies, *Deputado* Ulysses Guimarães. Indeed, it was not the natural inclination of the Itamaraty to pursue the policy to this extent, for it preferred to ease tensions with the US – especially at a time when the new Brazilian government was having to negotiate terms of repayment on its foreign debt – and the computer market reserve certainly did not do that. But the computer *corpo técnico* had been so successful in convincing members of the PMDB to support the policy that the Itamaraty had no alternative but to accept what even President Sarney, who as a senator had not been a strong supporter (some say he opposed it), now advocated enthusiastically.[32]

For the first meeting between the US negotiating team and the representatives from the Itamaraty, the PMDB had even wanted to send some of the party's closest allies to the computer *corpo técnico*, Cristina Tavares and another *deputado*, but the Itamaraty objected and at the last minute they stayed home. While there were some high-level meetings among top Brazilian policymakers to discuss what position the government would take, during which opponents of the market reserve voiced their objections, President Sarney refused to overturn the policy. It was significant that by this time the *corpo técnico* had allies in high positions within the new Ministry of Science and Technology (MCT). Luciano Coutinho, the MCT's Secretary-General, a loyal PMDB member and strong market reserve supporter, had become a close confidant to the president on computer matters at this time.[33]

THE BREAKDOWN OF THE PMDB AND PRESIDENT COLLOR'S NEW INDUSTRIAL POLICY

The computer *corpo técnico*'s successes – relative, at least, to the outcomes in the pharmaceutical industry, as Chapter 3 will show – continued through the era of the Constituent Assembly (1987–8), when Brazil's new civilian regime constitution was created, and on into the presidential campaigns of 1989 and the arrival, in March, 1990, of the Collor Administration. With the worsening economic situation during this period, the ruling PMDB party became increasingly discredited. By the time of the presidential election, presidential candidates were scrambling to distance themselves from President Sarney's failed Administration and from the PMDB as a whole. Fernando Collor, a 39-year-old governor of the tiny and impoverished state of Alagoas, won on the basis of his promises to cut inflation and to do away with the "*marajás*," unproductive, highly paid, and politically well-connected bureaucrats on the government payroll.[34]

Upon taking office, Collor's commitment to neoliberal economic policies became very clear. Among other measures, he sought the immediate withdrawal of the computer market reserve. Other neoliberals, realizing that little benefit would result from a sudden dismantling of the market reserve, might have been willing to change the policy gradually. This, however, was not Collor's approach. He was firmly committed to eliminating the policy as quickly as possible, as he had stated repeatedly during his presidential campaign.

Because of the computer *corpo técnico*'s earlier success in establishing the *Lei de Informática*, however, Collor was able to obtain only a gradual and partial withdrawal of the reserve.[35] Having institutionalized the policies it favored in the National Congress, the computer *corpo técnico* was better equipped than the pharmaceutical *corpo técnico* to resist Collor's new industrial policies (as will be demonstrated in the next chapter). Nevertheless, as other industrial sectors' needs for computers grew, the computer *corpo técnico*'s effectiveness was beginning to decline. The local protected industry's inability to produce computer goods of the same quality and price as those of its international competitors began to provoke widespread dissatisfaction with the computer market reserve, a phenomenon that no amount of lobbying on the part of the *corpo técnico* seemed likely to stop.

3   The pharmaceutical industry

The pharmaceutical industry's fate was far different from that of the computer industry. Political support for this sector during both the military era and the democratic transition period was weak, despite some efforts at various times to counteract this trend. This relative lack of political support for the sector continued with the Collor Administration. This chapter describes these relatively low levels of political support for the pharmaceutical industry, and to some extent explains them. The most important part of the explanation, however, will come in Chapter 4.

During the military regime, efforts to support the pharmaceutical industry came, in typically authoritarian fashion, from the top down in the form of new government directives and plans. Like the computer *corpo técnico* (at least in the early years of the military era), the pharmaceutical *corpo técnico* during this period essentially had to accept and cooperate with what the military itself decreed. Unlike its computer counterpart, however, the pharmaceutical *corpo técnico* did not succeed in promoting a forceful agenda of its own for change in the sector as the democratic transition got under way.

The pharmaceutical *corpo técnico* was weaker politically than its counterpart in the computer industry. Those few prominent and active *corpo técnico* members fighting for measures to benefit the national pharmaceutical sector came primarily from the *técnicos* segment of this group, not from the *empresários*, who had been so crucial to the successes of the computer *corpo técnico*. Most important, however, was that the pharmaceutical *corpo técnico* was not fully able to take advantage of the shift in government political orientation the democratic transition was bringing about.[1] As Chapter 4 will explain, the pharmaceutical *corpo técnico* was not able to do this to the extent the computer *corpo técnico* did, because of – in addition to the low degree of access – its relative lack of political affinity with the increasingly powerful PMDB politicians.

Central to any account of levels of government support during the military years is the creation of the *Central de Medicamentos* (CEME); for the democratic transition period, discussion of the *Programa Nacional da Indústria Farmacêutica* (Profarma) is key. Accordingly, the section of this chapter on the military era describes the level of government political support for the pharmaceutical *corpo técnico*'s programs in terms of its support for CEME. The section on the democratic transition describes the level of government political support primarily in terms of its support for Profarma.

THE MILITARY ERA

Foremost among the military government's efforts for the pharmaceutical industry – and certainly the zenith of its expression of concern – was the creation of the *Central de Medicamentos* (CEME), originally conceived as a combination of state enterprise producing generic pharmaceutical products at low cost, and a distribution center for pharmaceutical goods to the poor. Founded in 1976, during the Medici Administration, CEME was one facet of that government's attempts to deal, at least cosmetically, with the issues of the disparity of wealth and the health problems of the poor in Brazil. CEME's origins went back, as well, to a military study that indicated the need for an indigenous pharmaceutical industry in the event of war. Thus, even the pharmaceutical industry had some link to the Brazilian military's broad view of national security.

Those few members of the pharmaceutical *corpo técnico* who did fight for greater political support for the sector played up this aspect of the industry at every opportunity. Of course, such opportunities were considerably rarer during the military era. But while the National Congress remained open (serving, for the most part, as a sort of rubber stamp to the Executive Branch), expert witnesses – *corpo técnico* members – were sometimes called to provide their views about what should be done with the sector. The notable example during the military years was the 1980 hearings in the *Câmara dos Deputados* of the Investigating Committee on the Pharmaceutical Industry. At these hearings, a number of experts spoke about the need for national security reasons for a strong, viable, indigenous pharmaceutical industry.[2]

Ultimately, though, CEME was also a means to support the Brazilian pharmaceutical industry, because it bought products from Brazilian firms for later redistribution to the poor at low cost. One source argues (or at least strongly implies) that, in addition, CEME's real purpose was to expand the market share of private Brazilian and transnational pharmaceutical firms (Bertero 1972). By providing greater access to pharmaceutical products to greater numbers of people, CEME might eventually enable the private firms to take over portions of the newly created market.

With the benefit of hindsight, these claims seem somewhat dubious. Indeed, the whole conception of a state-run firm, and indeed of government intervention in general, was anathema to the transnational corporations (unless the intervention clearly served their interests). And at the time CEME was created, the government took great pains to assure pharmaceutical firms that the state-run CEME was not intended to be a competitor for their markets; it was meant to be more of an administrative center for distribution of drugs to people who otherwise would not be able to buy them ("ABIF..." 1971:10). Nevertheless, part of CEME's original mission did include promotion of indigenous research and development by channelling funds to local firms involved in such activities, and it did have a research and development department of its own ("ABIF..." 1971:10). Theoretically, CEME did have the potential to develop into some sort of national champion for the domestic pharmaceutical industry, as some of the more nationalist members of the pharmaceutical *corpo técnico* hoped that it would (more on this later).

In any case, the private firms – or at least the transnationals – feared CEME, and were not sufficiently reassured by the government pronouncements that they need not feel threatened. And by 1979, only three years after the presidential decree authorizing CEME's existence had been promulgated, the agency was restructured, its responsibilities being distributed among several government agencies. CEME was weakened in the process, its prospects for becoming a powerful instrument to combat denationalization shattered. Whether those officials in the military regime with ultimate authority over the agency sought to bring about this result or not, CEME could no longer pose a credible threat as a potential competitor to the private (or at least, to the private transnational) firms.

In the early years of CEME's existence some *corpo técnico* members had, indeed, had visions of CEME becoming a "Medibrás" along the lines of the large, powerful Petrobrás, a highly profitable state-run enterprise. The idea was to use CEME as a means to overcome the severe denationalization of the pharmaceutical sector. After 1979, however, the prospects of CEME's becoming a "Medibrás" were virtually nonexistent.

Evans claims that the government was disinclined to permit CEME to continue to represent even a potential threat to the private pharmaceutical industry, which by the late 1970s was already overwhelmingly dominated by the TNCs, because President Costa e Silva had close ties to the American DuPont Corporation (Evans 1979). Regardless of what made the government decide, in its restructuring of CEME, to decrease political support for the sector, the fact remains that the dismembering of CEME represented a definitive pulling back in what had appeared to be a "brief shining moment" of increased political support.

That the government could do this so decisively, by presidential decree, without debate over the matter, and that there was nothing the pharmaceutical *corpo técnico* (far weaker, anyway, than its counterpart in the computer industry) could do about it, demonstrates how industrial policy was made during the authoritarian era. It also demonstrates the pharmaceutical *corpo técnico*'s low degree of access to policymakers. For all the attempts on the part of some of the more activist and imaginative *corpo técnico* members to draw a tight linkage between development of a viable indigenous pharmaceutical industry and national security, and even after some within the military had made that linkage, the connection was sufficiently tenuous that when another strong element working within the military government – the goal of increased overall levels of foreign investment – conflicted with pushing for a stronger domestic pharmaceutical sector, actions that could be perceived as being hostile to the latter goals quickly were abandoned.

The *empresários* in the pharmaceutical sector can be faulted, in their failure even to attempt to support CEME to a greater extent than they did, for lack of vision. If anything, a CEME more capable of promoting indigenous research and development might have proved a greater boon to the local firms. Certain individuals within the *técnicos* segment of the pharmaceutical *corpo técnico*, however, especially given the context of the authoritarian regime in which they had to operate, sometimes took great risks to defend CEME and advance a more compelling agenda for the sector.

For example, even after the events of 1979, *técnicos* in CEME, with the money they saved by buying medications in bulk at cheap prices, still managed to channel 5 percent of CEME's total operating budget to R&D – despite the fact that funding for R&D was not authorized by the military authorities. The willingness of the *técnicos* providing this clandestine funding to risk punishment from the military in itself shows their determination of this segment of the *corpo téchnico* to keep indigenous technological research going (Pereira 1989; CEME 1988:2)[3].

Another important example of a *técnico* who risked his career to defend CEME was José Felicio Scardua, a president of the organization who was fired for his efforts. Extremely critical of the high dependence of the Brazilian pharmaceutical sector on foreign technology, Scardua – a strong promoter, incidentally, of the Profarma program, which sought to deal with this issue – had been critical of the government's lackadaisical approach to the problem. As the conservative newspaper *Estado de São Paulo* put it, Scardua was "dismissed for disagreeing with the current economic policy of the government and criticizing the total foreign dependence of the sector" ("Presidente..." 1984). Thus was industrial policy made – in a sector with a very low degree of access, at least – during the authoritarian period.[4]

Finally, some university professors, the third segment of the *corpo técnico*, were not as active in defending CEME as they would be later in supporting the Profarma program; again, however, given the context of the times, there was probably not much they could do anyway. One professor who did stand out, however, was Mario Victor de Assis Pacheco, a professor of medicine at the *Universidade Federal do Rio de Janeiro* (UFRJ). It was Pacheco who had advocated the idea of CEME becoming a "Medibrás." A strong critic of the practices of the transnational corporations in the pharmaceutical sector, he wrote several books ("Medication Mafia," "The Abuses of the Pharmaceutical Transnationals," "The Pharmaceutical Industry and National Security," etc.) attacking the foreign firms and calling for nationalization of the industry. Despite his extreme views, Pacheco was able to frame his arguments in such a way – note the title of his 1969 book (written during the height of the military regime), "The Pharmaceutical Industry and National Security" – that his respect among government officials was very high. In fact, he was one of the most prominent representatives of the pharmaceutical *corpo técnico* called as a witness to the *Câmara dos Deputados* hearings on the industry in 1980.

Nevertheless, the pharmaceutical *corpo técnico*, such as it was, could operate only within a highly circumscribed framework of action during the early military years. As the long, gradual transition to democracy began to open up new possibilities for action, however, only some elements within the pharmaceutical *corpo técnico* were able – or had the inclination – to rise to the occasion. The pharmaceutical *corpo técnico*'s efforts with respect to the Profarma plan and related efforts, to be discussed at length in the next section, demonstrate the limits of its capabilities even under what would seem to have been more favorable circumstances.

DEMOCRATIC TRANSITION AND BEYOND

The two *corpos técnicos* had very different responses to the changes that were occurring in the Brazilian National Congress at the beginning of the 1980s. When the Congress began to play an important role as an arena for the democratic movement, the computer *corpo técnico* actively sought to link itself to this movement and to the increasingly powerful PMDB. The pharmaceutical *corpo técnico*, on the other hand, took a much more passive role. Because its different political characteristics did not give it (as with computers) a strong political affinity with the PMDB politicians, the pharmaceutical *corpo técnico* made few efforts to link itself to the new political forces within Brazil.

While the computer *corpo técnico* set the agenda to such an extent that the PMDB embraced its plans wholeheartedly and perhaps normally dubious *militares* in the PDS felt compelled to go along, the pharmaceutical *corpo técnico* was far less successful. While advancing an initially ambitious proposal that sought to impose some broad market reserve measures for the industry, the pharmaceutical *corpo técnico* managed to have only an extremely weakened version adopted. Pharmaceutical *corpo técnico* members, politically very different from their counterparts in the computer industry, were unable to carry out the kind of activist, full-blown lobbying campaign in the Brazilian Congress that was so successful for the computer *corpo técnico*. They lacked the inclination and the ability to link their interests with the new trends in Brazilian politics.

At about the same time that the computer *corpo técnico* was beginning to approach the PMDB politicians, some of the more activist members within the pharmaceutical *corpo técnico* were advancing a proposal, known as *Programa Nacional da Indústria Farmacêutica* (Profarma), that would promote their sector's political interests as well. Profarma's purpose was to reduce external dependence in the sector by means of import restrictions for certain products, increased funding for research, etc. That the proposal was never really implemented, at least in the way it was originally intended, reveals just how weak the pharmaceutical *corpo técnico* really was.

Announced in November, 1982, the Profarma plan was significant not only for its overall importance, but because like CEME it, too, began with much higher expectations and broader goals than it achieved in the end. Unlike the CEME case, however, this "watering down" of the Profarma plan took place in the context of Brazil's democratic transition. That the pharmaceutical *corpo técnico* was unable to make use of that transition, which provided it with more favorable circumstances under which to work than those the computer *corpo técnico* faced, suggests that the relative lack of political affinity between the pharmaceutical *corpo técnico* and key politicians in the PMDB played an important role in determining outcomes.

As noted, the Profarma proposal arose at about the same time, late 1982, that the computer market reserve's advocates were beginning to lobby the PMDB. Unlike the case of the computer industry, however, the impetus for the proposal came as a top-down initiative from the executive branch of government. Furthermore, in the Profarma case, discussion and debate about the proposal remained at the elite level of government ministers and technocrats.[5] Finally, the proposal became stalled by bickering among the five ministers charged with the authority to approve the plan. Unlike the computer *corpo técnico*, which had approached the PMDB as early as 1979, the pharmaceutical *corpo técnico* made no real effort to lobby the increasingly important PMDB until much later, and certainly did not have a large-scale lobbying effort in place to win eventual legislative approval for such a program in the National Congress. Thus, the pharmaceutical *corpo técnico* did not take advantage of the strategy the computer *corpo técnico* had used so successfully to seek support and legitimacy for its own programs.

Indeed, what set plans for Profarma in motion initially was not independent actions in the part of the *corpo técnico* – and certainly not on the part of the *empresários* in the sector, as had been the case with computers – but rather the Planning Secretary's concerns about the severe negative balance of payments Brazil was running in the pharmaceutical sector. Realizing that something had to be done to reduce Brazil's approximately 302 million (US dollars) annual expenditures on imported raw materials[6] for manufacturing pharmaceutical products, Planning Minister Antonio Delfim Netto called a meeting of *empresários* from the sector and urged them to formulate some kind of plan to overcome the problem ("Indústria de remédios..." 1982; "Indústria farmacêutica..." 1982). Stressing the crisis nature of the situation, Delfim Netto issued an "ultimatum" to the industry to come up with the plan within eight to ten days.

The initial response from the pharmaceutical industry in Brazil, including the transnational corporations, was highly favorable. About 70 firms expressed interest in taking part in the effort to increase national production of *matérias-primas*. Of these 70 firms, however, only about 20 percent were genuinely Brazilian firms; the rest were transnationals which hoped to benefit from government incentives for national production of the primary ingredients ("Indústria farmacêutica..." 1982). The president of Abifarma, an organization that represented the interests of the transnational corporations in Brazil, was as enthusiastic about the plan as was José Felicio Scardua, who – as president of CEME and a highly active lobbyist for greater domestic manufacture of *matérias-primas* – was a prominent member of the pharmaceutical *corpo técnico*.

While the new endeavor's broad goals (reducing dependence on foreign technology, increasing domestic production of primary ingredients) were defined relatively quickly, the specific proposals remained to be determined. By the beginning of 1983, these had taken shape, and the more definitive plan continued to be known as Profarma. With the development of the more concrete proposals, however, the unity between domestic and transnational segments of the industry dissolved. *Técnicos* in CEME, in the Council of Industrial Development (CDI), and in the Secretariat of Industrial Technology (STI) – essentially the entire *técnicos* segment of the pharmaceutical *corpo técnico* – had come up with the proposals, and had advanced a more nationalist version than the transnationals could tolerate.

The problem the foreign firms saw with the Profarma proposals centered around key provisions that limited the participation of transnational corporations in the Brazilian pharmaceutical industry. Specifically, these firms were vehemently opposed to provisions that sought to increase domestic production of primary ingredients by means of financial incentives and import restrictions, "by firms of national capital and with effective national control" ("Mudança..." 1983). Yet this very provision for *national* firms was what the entire program was about. To give in to the transnationals on this point would, in effect, nullify the Profarma's ability to carry out its goals of – precisely – increasing internal production of primary ingredients by national firms, and reducing dependence on foreign technology.

The transnationals, however, held a powerful bargaining chip: they could appeal to their home countries, currently in the process of negotiating Brazil's foreign debt, to intervene on their behalf. And indeed, representatives of the British, German, and North American commercial interests in Brazil, as well as the president of Abifarma, sent angry telexes to the President of the Republic as well as to the five government ministers with authority to approve the Profarma, implying precisely this. As the text of the German telegram stated: "the [Profarma] program, if implemented in its current conception, would constitute, without doubt, a permanent obstacle to Germany's international economic relations with Brazil" ("Crescem..." 1983). The British and American telegrams made essentially the same point.

The possibility of a strain in economic relations, at precisely the time when Brazil was engaged in delicate financial negotiations with these countries, terrified those government ministers responsible for renegotiating the debt. Ironically enough, these ministers included the Minister of Planning, Delfim Netto – the same official who, only the year before, had issued the ultimatum to the industry to come up with something like Profarma – as well as the Minister of Finance, Ernane Galveas. Both of these officials were also among the five charged with the responsibility (in this time before the National Congress had much authority) of approving the Profarma proposal. (The other three were the Minister of Social Welfare, the Minister of Health, and the Minister of Industry and Commerce.) Perhaps inevitably, given what these ministers perceived to be the consequences of antagonizing the TNCs (as well as Graham Allison's dictum that "where you stand depends upon where you sit"), the Minister of Planning and the Minister of Finance opposed the strong version of the Profarma proposal, and refused to approve it without alterations. The other three ministers, influenced by their advisers among the pharmaceutical *corpo técnico* (e.g., José Felicio Scardua), approved it without any changes.[7]

Thus began the long and tortuous process of attempting to alter the Profarma proposal to get unanimous approval. Some of the more activist members of the pharmaceutical *corpo técnico* made an effort to support the program as originally conceived, or at least to push for greater political support from the government for national firms. Despite these efforts, the pharmaceutical *corpo técnico*, weaker than its counterpart in the computer industry and facing more entrenched opposition from the long-established transnational pharmaceutical firms, ultimately gave in. After three years of attempting to obtain approval from all of the minsters concerned, the pharmaceutical *corpo técnico* gave up, in effect, on the original conception of

Profarma. Some kind of program for the pharmaceutical industry – no longer named Profarma – was approved in late 1984.[8] In this final form, however, the force of the original Profarma provisions was so greatly altered and diminished that the original vision from which it had sprung had become virtually unrecognizable. For instance, all financial incentives to be given to national firms would now also be given to foreign firms as well. The numerous changes had so watered down the original provisions of the proposal that it had become almost irrelevant.

Clearly, the strength of the TNCs and their allies within Brazil help explain the fate of the Profarma program. Unlike the case with the computer industry, in the pharmaceutical sector the TNCs had dominated the Brazilian market since the end of World War II. Hence, when the government made some effort to enact policies to overcome this situation, it met extremely fierce opposition from the TNCs.

But another important factor in explaining Profarma's demise was the political characteristics of the pharmaceutical *corpo técnico* itself. In fact, some individual members of the pharmaceutical *corpo técnico* could very well be described as activists for the Profarma cause (overturning Brazil's dependence in the pharmaceutical sector by such measures as a selected market reserve for certain *matérias-primas*, and special incentives to aid genuinely national firms). But never was there the kind of broadly based support for such activity among all members of the pharmaceutical *corpo técnico* that the computer *corpo técnico* enjoyed. The impetus for the Profarma proposal itself came not from the *empresários* in the sector, who tended to be fairly apolitical, but rather from the *técnicos*. Even the *técnicos* had differences among themselves that prevented strong solidarity about what political course of action to take.

Of course, some *empresários* did speak up in favor of the proposal. For instance, some national manufacturers grouped together to form the Association of National Laboratories (Alanac), an organization designed to represent the interests of the approximately 300 primarily national firms in the pharmaceutical industry. One of Alanac's first acts was to send a telex to President Figueiredo and the five ministers responsible for approving the Profarma, expressing support for the plan and emphasizing the importance of support from the Ministers of Planning and Finance ("Indústria farmacêutica..." 1983). Kurt Politzer, a prominent *empresário* and director of the important Brazilian firm *Guanabara Técnica e Industrial* (Getec) – which at that time wanted to nationalize production of Vitamin C – also spoke out in favor of the proposal. In fact, he went so far as to state that "it is essential, for the national firms of the pharmaceutical sector, that a market reserve be created" ("Galveas..." 1983). (Politzer's status in the industry was evidenced somewhat later by his being one of the key *empresários* to advise the New Republic transition team on a new industrial policy after the 1985 election.)[9]

At no time, however, did any of these *empresários* try to organize an extensive lobbying campaign of the type the computer *corpo técnico* created. Alanac, while meant to be a lobbying organization of sorts, was most concerned with a relatively narrow political agenda: maintaining Brazil's policy of not recognizing patents for pharmaceutical products. Certainly it did not, as did Edson Fregni's *Movimento Brasil de Informática*, call for extended rights for Brazilian indians and try to link itself to the *Diretas Já!* campaign. And Kurt Politzer later backed away from any proposals that mentioned any kind of market reserve, which was, in part, what Profarma was.[10] This timid response can be explained in part by the fact that Politzer's firm, like many other Brazilian firms in the sector, was a joint venture with foreign firms, which themselves opposed Profarma.

The *técnicos* were more active and bolder politically than the *empresários*. Yet, as mentioned, the *técnicos* soon began to engage in bureaucratic squabbles among themselves, thus making even this segment of the *corpo técnico* relatively ineffective in the effort to develop and support a cohesive plan for the sector. Unlike the computer industry's *técnicos,* united into one cohesive agency, SEI, *técnicos* in the pharmaceutical industry lacked a strong, cohesive institutional base. This situation sometimes led to serious conflicts among the different agencies charged with making and implementing policy.

For example, CEME was responsible for buying, distributing, and – to some extent – manufacturing the government's supplies of pharmaceutical products, most of which were provided to the poor at low cost. It also funded some indigenous research and development efforts. The *Conselho de Desenvolvimento Industrial* (CDI) was responsible for deciding which foreign firms could form joint ventures in Brazil and under what conditions. This division of responsibilities created some problems between the two agencies. As the Vice President for Planning at CEME said in an interview, the *técnicos* in charge of the pharmaceutical sector at the CDI were corrupt and often looked the other way about such things as superprofiting, a practice in which the subsidiaries of the TNCs would buy equipment and basic ingredients from the home office at prices high above their true value. In this way the TNCs could avoid paying taxes on remitted earnings and get around requirements for reinvestment of a certain percentage of the profits.[11]

It did seem unusual that a highly placed *técnico* at the CDI, in charge of deciding which foreign investments in pharmaceuticals the government would approve, did not have a set list of guidelines to follow but decided case by case.[12] But whether or not *técnicos* in the CDI were corrupt was less significant than the fact that important *técnicos* in CEME thought they were.

This showed that there was a great deal of conflict, mistrust, etc. even within the *técnicos* part of the *corpo técnico*. University professors showed a lack of consensus similar to that of the *técnicos* and *empresários*. The sector did have strong supporters from this segment of the *corpo técnico*. For instance, following in the tradition of Pacheco de Assis, Geraldo Giovanni, a professor of sociology at the *Universidade Estadual de Campinas* (Unicamp), was an especially forceful proponent of strong state action – specifically, implementation of the Profarma proposal – to combat the dominance of the TNCs in the pharmaceutical industry. Giovanni's book, *A Questão dos Remédios no Brasil*, remains one of the most frequently cited works in any article or study on the pharmaceutical industry. Like Pacheco de Assis, Giovanni, too, quickly developed a reputation as an expert on the industry's problems and was present at virtually all of the most important debates and panel discussions on the subject (Giovanni 1987).[13]

Other professors were also willing to support the Profarma program. When the government announced in June 1983 that the Profarma would be altered so that all firms, not just those of "national capital and effective national control" would be able to participate in the financial incentives and other benefits of the program, 60 professors from the Chemistry Institute of Unicamp (one of Brazil's best research universities) and the Brazilian Chemistry Society signed a joint letter expressing their concern about the strong influence of Abifarma and the transnational corporations in bringing the alteration about. Such a modification would defeat the purpose of a program that sought to benefit genuinely national firms, argued the professors. After all, the national firms were the ones that needed assistance, because of the domestic chemical-pharmaceutical sector's severe dependence on foreign technology. The sector imported 85 percent of the primary ingredients used, the equivalent of US$365 million per year. Moreover, "of the approximately 600 firms in the sector,[14] 520 were national and 80 multinational, but the latter account[ed] for 80 percent of the sector's gross profits" ("Participação..." 1983).

But unlike the university professors in the computer *corpo técnico*, who along with their *técnico* and *empresário* colleagues held similar views, the professors of the pharmaceutical *corpo técnico* were unable to coalesce around a common stance toward policies such as the Profarma program. Indeed, José Barberio, one of the most important of these professors because of his position as Director of Pharmaceutical Sciences at the *Universidade de São Paulo* (USP), publicly opposed any policy that would limit involvement of foreign pharmaceutical firms in the Brazilian market. Barberio wrote in an editorial on the Profarma proposal," as much as one might criticize the actions of these [foreign] firms, the benefits they bring surpass by far any possible inconvenience" (Barberio 1983).

The result of this disunity and relative lack of political activism by the different parts of the *corpo técnico* was a half-hearted lobbying effort. This allowed the administrative elites to maintain control of the decisionmaking process, which, in effect, kept the Profarma proposal from being approved.

The weakest aspect of the pharmaceutical *corpo técnico*'s lobbying effort was its failure to bring the proposal before the National Congress, as the computer *corpo técnico* had done with the market reserve. As a result, the proposal had to be approved by five government ministers before it could become law. As already pointed out, two of the five, Finance Minster Ernane Galveas and Planning Secretary Antonio Delfim Netto, had strong disagreements with certain measures within the proposal. Specifically, these two ministers objected to provisions that would forbid joint ventures with foreign firms. Concerned about antagonizing important foreign firms from creditor nations in the midst of Brazil's debt negotiations, Galveas and Delfim Netto, in effect, vetoed the proposal. In contrast, after the computer *corpo técnico*'s extremely effective appeals to the National Congress, that whole body would have been in an uproar if something like that had happened with, say, the *Lei de Informática*.

THE NEW REPUBLIC: THE EARLY YEARS

The differences between outcomes for the computer and pharmaceutical *corpos técnicos* continued after the transition to the democratic New Republic government in 1985. For the first year, at least, the shift in government seemed to bode well for the pharmaceutical *corpo técnico*'s agenda and for the pharmaceutical industry as a whole. By 1986, however – the very same year that President Sarney was refusing to give in to international pressures to do away with the computer market reserve – the pharmaceutical *corpo técnico*'s relative lack of influence over the PMDB was evident again. Specifically, the government acquiesced to international pressures to quash new proposals (emerging this time in the National Congress) for a market reserve in the pharmaceutical sector.

The 1985 transition to civilian rule had raised expectations greatly in the pharmaceutical industry, at least among that more nationalist and activist segment of it – the *técnicos* – who once again rose to the fore in an effort to bring about radical change.[15] The *técnicos* sensed that they might now be better able to justify their programs under this new government, with all of its rhetoric about "new social priorities" and "everything for the social welfare."[16] In any event, it seemed that the new government would find it more difficult to resist proposals for more support for key projects and programs when the *técnicos* phrased them in terms of "improving the social welfare of the Brazilian population," etc. The *técnicos'* successes in 1985 were promising. Tancredo Neves, the civilian president-elect, had met with key *corpo técnico* members and had already decided on a number of programs for the sector.[17] Although Neves died before he could take office, Sarney, the Vice-President who assumed power, continued – at least for a time – to adhere to a shift in social priorities, developing such legislation as the Program for Social Priorities, and more financial support for the pharmaceutical sector in the First National Development Plan of the New Republic. As CEME's 1988 annual report stated, "with the advent of the social policy of the Sarney government, CEME received large government resources."[18] Some successes continued on into the period (1987) of the Constituent Assembly, when CEME managed finally to make official the 5 percent of its budget targeted for R&D.[19] CEME also managed to get other measures favorable to the pharmaceutical industry, but of a more general nature, approved for inclusion in the new Brazilian constitution.[20]

Despite these successes, overall outcomes for the pharmaceutical *corpo técnico* after 1985 did demonstrate low levels of government political support. Proposals to establish a market reserve, which emerged in 1986 from the Minister of Industry and Commerce as well as from the National Congress, met with the same international pressures the Profarma had faced.[21] As before, these pressures were victorious. Ultimately, President Sarney vetoed one such proposal that actually had been passed in the National Congress. As one US trade negotiator, involved with the computer market reserve negotiations, remarked, the timing for the pharmaceutical proposal could not have been worse, coming up for presidential approval in the same week that the Brazilian government was meeting with the US to discuss the computer market reserve ("EUA..." 1986).

THE BREAKDOWN OF PMDB AND PRESIDENT COLLOR'S NEW INDUSTRIAL POLICY

As mentioned earlier, the different outcomes of the two *corpos técnicos* continued through the Collor Administration. Able to obtain only the gradual withdrawal of the computer market reserve, Collor succeeded in completely eliminating talk of any similar plans for the pharmaceutical sector. Moreover, the policy that for 20 years had been the very centerpiece of the pharmaceutical *corpo técnico*'s political agenda – the non-recognition of patents for pharmaceutical products – was quickly overturned. The members of the pharmaceutical *corpo técnico* clearly had fared worse than their counterparts in the computer industry.

4 Political characteristics of the *corpos técnicos*

The differences in political orientation between the computer *corpo técnico* and its pharmaceutical counterpart are instructive. The computer *corpo técnico* was made up of relatively left-leaning, politically active individuals; the pharmaceutical *corpo técnico*, on the other hand, was composed of relatively conservative, politically inert members. This chapter seeks to demonstrate these differences by means of a detailed examination of the political characteristics of the two *corpos técnicos*.

There are a number of ways systematically to assess the extent of the political differences between the two respective *corpos técnicos*. Survey data is useful in providing a broad scope. But because of the nature of the phenomenon to be examined here – the special ability of an elite group of individuals to influence key politicians – detailed analysis of select members of the elite *corpos técnicos* is especially useful. Such analysis supplies context and a wealth of detail that broad surveys cannot possibly capture. For this reason, this chapter makes use of some general survey data but emphasizes in-depth, individual analysis of select *corpo técnico* members.

Before considering the survey data and discussing individual cases, this chapter will examine broader aspects of *corpo técnico* membership. Specifically, we will look at the manner of recruitment into the *corpos técnicos,* giving special attention to such matters as educational background of *corpo técnico* members, extent to which *empresário corpo técnico* members were entrepreneurs versus heirs to the family firm, and differences in generational factors between the two *corpos técnicos'* members. We will argue that all of these factors were important in determining political characteristics.

CORPO TÉCNICO RECRUITMENT

Educational background

Many scholars have documented the phenomenon, common throughout

Latin America, of the high degree of political involvement on the part of intellectuals (Walker 1967:408–30). This phenomenon occurred, in part, because those with the extensive education required to become members of the intellectual, educated elite were comparatively rare in Latin America. Hence, such individuals not only had more credibility but also tended to feel a greater obligation, relative to their counterparts in, say, the United States, to become involved in political issues.

In addition, and related to this first point, the intellectual, educated elite in Latin America definitely tended toward the "liberal" or "left" end of the political spectrum. Such political issues as widespread poverty, the need for land reform, and the inegalitarian distribution of the benefits of rapid economic growth, all loomed especially large in the region, and those who had special abilities to do something about such problems – if not on a technical, immediate level, then by means of action in the political sphere – could not help but have their attention drawn to these issues on a constant, daily basis.

All of this, combined with a political culture and tradition based not on individualism and corresponding notions of "every man for himself," but rather on a more feudal, patronage kind of ideology, worked to make the intellectuals in Brazil and the rest of Latin America politically very active, involved, and, on the whole, moderately leftist or "liberal." And certainly, the intellectuals as a whole were strong supporters of democratic, civilian rule.

Results from the survey[1] support these assertions. Of all *corpo técnico* members from both sectors, 56 percent of those with relatively high levels of education (graduate work in Brazil or abroad) described themselves as "extreme left," "moderate left," or "center left," while only 24 percent of those with relatively low levels of education (university graduate or below) described themselves in this way.[2] The chi square statistic for these results, .003, suggests that the probability of this correlation being due merely to "chance" is only three out of a thousand – in other words, highly unlikely.

For those who had obtained advanced postgraduate degrees abroad, and thus stood at the pinnacle of this elite group (in the survey, 36 percent of computer *corpo técnico* members versus 20 percent of pharmaceutical *corpo técnico* members had done graduate work at foreign universities), this tendency was even more accentuated.[3] Moreover, most members of the computer *corpo técnico* who had done graduate work abroad had taken their advanced degrees between the mid-1960s and early 1970s at universities such as Wisconsin, Berkeley, Stanford, and MIT in the US, Sussex in the UK, and the University of Paris in France – institutions which, at that time, were being swept by the radical student movements of the era. (Student activism was taking place in Brazil, as well, but these were the harshest years of the military regime, when universities were often closed down, and student radicals were tortured and imprisoned – thus putting a damper, to say the least, on such activity.) Many of the elite members of the *corpo técnico* who attended these universities were affected by the experience, as we will explain in more detail below.

Of course, while having attended an elite graduate school abroad at a particular time does seem to be correlated with a certain kind of political orientation – above all, with strong support for democratic government – it was not necessarily the graduate study itself that created such political views. It is important to keep in mind that only a particular kind of student – the "best and the brightest" – was likely to undertake graduate study overseas in the first place. Such people, as we have already argued, would tend (at least in Latin America) to be more inclined toward "democratic" views in any case.

Business ownership

Empresários (business owners) were a crucial element of the *corpo técnico* coalitions. They provided funds and political influence. Lindblom has documented some notable instances of the extent of special political influence business firms have in the United States.[4] This kind of special political influence on the part of business executives was especially strong in Brazil, where countervailing forces such as political parties, labor groups, and consumer associations were particularly weak.

But there was a difference in the way the business owners in the computer and pharmaceutical industries went about their lobbying. As Chapter 2 demonstrated, the computer owners were much more active politically from the beginning, and especially so as the transition to democracy gained momentum. As this chapter will argue throughout, part of this had to do with certain political characteristics of those attracted to the computer field in the first place. In addition, however, this characteristic had to do with the fact that the most politically active businessmen in the computer sector tended to be entrepreneurs, while businessmen in the pharmaceutical sector tended to be heirs to the family firm.[5] For the *corpos técnicos* as a whole, responses to this particular item on the survey would seem to support this assertion; approximately 91 percent of *empresários* in the computer *corpo técnico* indicated that they were founders or co-founders of their firms, while only 57 percent of the *empresários* in the pharmaceutical *corpo técnico* described themselves in these terms.[6] Of the most highly politically active *empresários* in the computer *corpo técnico* – Ricardo Saur, Mario Ripper, Edson Dytz, Edson Fregni, Milton Seligman – all were or became entrepreneurs who started their own firms. (Ivan da Costa Marques was a notable exception; we will discuss his case at greater length in a later section of this chapter.) In the pharmaceutical *corpo técnico*, in contrast (as already shown in Chapter 3), most politically active individuals were not *empresários* anyway, but tended to come from the *técnicos* portion of the *corpo técnico*. Notable exceptions, of course, were the *empresários* Kurt Politzer (as an entrepreneur, somewhat of an anomaly in this sector) and Adilson Xavier (more typically, heir to his family's firm). We will discuss Politzer's rather atypical case later in this chapter.

The difference between entrepreneurs and heirs has a basis in logic. Entrepreneurs, by their very definition, are willing to take risks. They have other essential characteristics as well. Because starting a new business requires an inordinate amount of energy, they tend to be energetic, active individuals.

Clearly, taking risks was what the entrepreneurs who made up the *empresário* part of the computer *corpo técnico* were doing as they began to align themselves with Brazil's democratic opposition movement, the *Movimento Democrático Brasileiro* (MDB), which later became the main opposition party, the PMDB. It was what electrical engineer and computer entrepreneur Edson Fregni was doing when he shouted *Diretas Já!* (Direct Elections Now!) at the conclusion of his speech to various military personnel at an award banquet in 1983. And the computer *corpo técnico*'s whole campaign in favor of the PMDB's version of the market reserve, the *Lei de Informática*, was conducted at a time when the regime was still emerging from that dark period when even uttering deprecating words against the President of the Republic might land the speaker in jail – where torture was common – for the offense.

In the pharmaceutical *corpo técnico*, the *empresários* were far more risk-averse. They made no such alignments with controversial political movements, no such controversial statements of any note. As shown in Chapter 3, those in the pharmaceutical *corpo técnico* who were willing to take such risks were the *técnicos* (such as José Felicio Scardua, former president of CEME, who was fired for his statements) and university professors (e.g., the highly controversial Mario Victor de Assis Pacheco). As we have seen, however, even these parts of the pharmaceutical *corpo técnico* were not unified in this regard.

The generational factor

The computer *corpo técnico* (or at least, the most highly educated, elite segment of it, which later went on to become especially politically active) came of age intellectually at elite American, British, and French universities in the late 1960s and early 1970s. The timing and locale of this intellectual coming of age facilitated the development of the distinctive political orientation these individuals shared. In Chapter 2 we have already referred to some of the characteristics that tended to go along with membership in this particular generation of youthful Brazilian intellectuals: a willingness to take risks, to question authority, and to tweak the set views of the "Establishment." The computer *corpo técnico* had these qualities in abundance. Edson Fregni and Milton Seligman were particularly relevant examples, and will be discussed at greater length in the last section of this chapter. But membership in the generation that came of age intellectually in the late 1960s/early 1970s was something virtually all of the key members of the computer *corpo técnico* shared. In addition to Fregni and Seligman, Ivan da Costa Marques, Ricardo Saur, Mario Ripper, José Ripper, and Claudio Mammana were all in their early 30s in the mid-to-late 1970s; and at this time, all had recently returned from graduate school in the US.[7] Fregni and Saur had been at Stanford; Claudio Mammana, to the University of Wisconsin at Madison; José Ripper (somewhat earlier, in the early sixties) to MIT; and Ivan da Costa Marques and Mario Ripper had been contemporaries at Berkeley, where they met often – all the while taking precautions to avoid any possible monitoring by the SNI, Brazil's equivalent to the FBI – to discuss the repressive political situation back home.

As noted, the pharmaceutical *corpo técnico* members did not do graduate work abroad to the extent that the key computer *corpo técnico* members did. Furthermore, as Chapter 3 demonstrated, and as the additional survey data in the next section indicates, they did not develop a shared political orientation to anywhere near the extent of their counterparts in the computer *corpo técnico*.

SURVEY DATA

We can now take a more in-depth look at additional survey data on the two *corpos técnicos.* Because the "political affinity" hypothesis argues that the political characteristics of the computer *corpo técnico* would be similar to those of the rising PMDB politicians – i.e., relatively "left" of center and vehemently pro-democratic – we will look particularly for evidence which tests this proposition.

In order to measure differences in the degree of left/right political orientation between the two *corpos técnicos,* one item on the survey questionnaire asked *corpo técnico* members to classify themselves on a spectrum of political attitudes. Respondents were given seven choices, from "extreme left" to "extreme right." Significantly, approximately 36 percent of the pharmaceutical *corpo técnico* respondents indicated that they considered their political attitudes to fall under the categories of either "moderate right" or "center right". (No one indicated extreme right.) In contrast, only about 9 percent of the computer *corpo técnico* respondents classified their political attitudes as falling into these categories. On the other hand, about 86 percent of the computer *corpo técnico* respondents did classify their political attitudes as either "moderate left", "center left", or "center" (admittedly a fairly wide range of choice), while only about 61 percent of the pharmaceutical *corpo técnico* respondents – even given the broad range of these three categories – indicated that their political attitudes conformed to these classifications.[8] And of course, these are percentages for the *corpo técnico* members as a whole; when one considers specifically the most active and influential *corpo técnico* members (particularly those from the computer *corpo técnico*), the differences between the *corpos técnicos* are even more pronounced.

Given that direct presidential elections were reinstated in Brazil only in 1989, following a 25–year absence during the military dictatorship, voting patterns among *corpo técnico* members also provide a useful indicator of political attitudes. The peculiar nature of the Brazilian presidential election process makes voting patterns for this country especially revealing. The process of selection of presidential candidates progressed through two rounds: in the first round (*primeiro turno*), voters chose from among 22 different candidates, representing a wide range of political views. The top two contenders in this first round went on to the second, or *segundo turno*. Thus, the way *corpo técnico* members voted in the *primeiro turno*, when they had the widest selection from which to choose, is the most indicative of their political views.

Of the 22–odd candidates[9] who campaigned in the first round, only about eight had sufficient following to be considered important candidates: Lula, Collor, Mario Covas, Brizola, Affif, Maluf, Ulysses Guimarães, and Roberto Freire. These eight can be grouped fairly easily according to relatively "leftist" and relatively "conservative" political leanings. The "leftists" would include Lula (Worker's Party); Mario Covas (Social Democratic Party); Brizola (Democratic Worker's Party); Roberto Freire (Communist Party); and Ulysses Guimarães (Democratic Movement Party). The "conservatives" would include Collor (National Renovation Party, but formerly of the military-related PDS party); Maluf (PDS); and Affif (Liberal Party).

As the argument advanced here would lead us to expect, computer *corpo técnico* respondents heavily favored "leftist" candidates (81 percent) over "conservative" ones (19 percent). Pharmaceutical *corpo técnico* respondents, on the other hand, were evenly divided in their preference for leftist (50 percent) or conservative candidates (50 percent).

The chi square value for these data indicates that the probability of the responses falling into these categories purely by chance is very small – just .01, lower than the .05 value that statisticians consider to be a conservative measure for a significant association between two variables. To put it another way, the probability that this apparent strong relationship between *corpo técnico* membership and choice of "leftist" versus "conservative" political candidate is merely accidental is one in a hundred. Thus, the computer *corpo técnico did* favor leftist candidates to a much greater extent than did the pharmaceutical *corpo técnico.*

Another highly relevant finding from the survey was the extent to which *corpo técnico* members from the respective industries participated in the *Diretas Já!* campaign. *Diretas Já!* (Direct Elections Now!) was a pro-democratic political movement in Brazil in the mid-1980s which called for reinstatement of direct presidential elections. The main political party in opposition to the military government, known first as the Brazilian Democratic Movement (MDB) and later as the Democratic Movement Party (PMDB), was the primary institution around which this movement organized. Clearly, the PMDB was the party on the rise in the 1980s; after the 1982 elections, it was dominant in the National Congress, and the first civilian president-elect after the 1985 presidential elections, Tancredo Neves, was a member of this party.[10] (Although Neves died before he could take office, the Executive officials he had appointed were mostly affiliated with *Diretas Ja!* and the PMDB.) Thus, the extent to which individuals from the respective *corpo técnicos* participated in the *Diretas Já!* movement helps indicate the extent of their political affinity with the dominant party.

Like political orientation of presidential candidates, level of support for the *Diretas Já!* campaign can also be divided into two categories, "high" and "low." In order to be placed in the "high" category, respondents had to indicate that they had supported *Diretas Já!* by either participating in demonstrations, speaking publicly to convince others to support the campaign, giving contributions of voluntary service, giving financial contributions, signing petitions, or doing any combination of the above. In order to be placed in the "low" category, respondents had to indicate that they had either given little support of any type to the movement, or had given no support whatsoever.

The finding in this instance was even more revealing about the differences in political characteristics between the two *corpos técnicos.* Of computer *corpo técnico* respondents, 65 percent had had "high" levels of participation in the *Diretas Já!* campaign, compared with only 28 percent of those in the pharmaceutical *corpo técnico.* In contrast, only 35 percent of the computer respondents had had "low" levels of participation in the movement, compared with 71 percent of those from the pharmaceutical sector. Considering again the chi square statistic, we find that the probability of these ratios being purely accidental is only .002, or two out of a thousand. These data certainly tend to support the hypothesis that individuals in the computer *corpo técnico* had a high level of political affinity with the PMDB politicians, while those in pharmaceutical *corpo técnico* did not.

Table 4.1 summarizes a few of the most salient political characteristics of the *corpos técnicos*.

Table 4.1   Political characteristics of the *corpos técnicos*

	Computers	Pharmaceuticals
Active *Diretas Já!* participation (%)	65	28
Support for "left" politicians (%)	81	50
"Right" self-identification (%)	9	36

REPRESENTATIVE CASES

These statistical data do give some sense of the overall situation. As mentioned, however, because the *corpos técnicos* were composed of a small, select elite, detailed, in-depth discussion of representative cases is more useful here than it might be where the sample size is very large. For each of the *corpos técnicos*, then, we will present individual case studies of those individuals who were especially prominent in the making of policy, or at least were designated as having an important lobbying/policymaking role.

Of course, even with the relatively small numbers of key policymakers/lobbyists within each *corpo técnico* (approximately 15–20 for the computer industry, and 10–15 for pharmaceuticals), it is not possible to examine every case.[11] Therefore, in order to give a sense of the nature of the more prominent policymakers within each of the *corpos técnicos*, we will simply list briefly, with titles, those who belonged to this more select group in the computer and pharmaceutical industries. Then we will go on to discuss in more detail representative cases of *empresários, técnicos,* and professors from each of the two industries.

In the computer *corpo técnico*, the most important members during the democratic transition period were Milton Seligman, adviser to various PMDB politicians during the crucial early 1980s period (currently founder of his own computer firm); Edson Fregni, President of the Brazilian Computers and Peripherals Manufacturers' Association (Abicomp) at various times since the late 1970s, founder of the *Movimento Brasil de Informática* (MBI), and founding president of Scopus Computers; Fernando Calicchio, the MBI's lobbyist since 1983 (and later its president); Arturo Pereira Nunes, former *técnico* at SEI and president of Abicomp; Edson Dytz, Executive Director of SEI during the democratic transition and current president of his own computer firm, Dytz Informática; and José Ezil Veiga da Rocha,

Executive Director of SEI during 1985–7, the period of the Constituent Assembly, when Brazil's new constitution was being written.

Those who played an especially important role during the early phase of the industry (the military period), and still had influence during the democratic transition phase, were: Ivan da Costa Marques, former Executive Director of CAPRE (precursor to SEI) and president of Cobra, the Brazilian state computer firm; Mario Ripper, also a founding member of CAPRE, and current Executive Director of Elebra Computers (one of the original members of the triple alliance of state, local, and transnational capital when the government began the program to develop the computer industry); Claudio Mammana, former head of Abicomp, currently Executive Director of his own computer firm and member of the Board of Directors of Abicomp; Ricardo Saur, the electrical engineer who teamed up with Frigate Captain Guaranys in the initial government project to fund a Brazilian computer, currently president of his own computer firm, and board member of Abicomp; José Ripper, brother of Mario Ripper, another former CAPRE member, and currently owner of his own telecommunications firm; and finally José Doria Porto, professor of electrical engineering and Director of the computer project at USP at the time Edson Fregni and Claudio Mammana were students there, and currently co-founder of his own computer firm.[12]

In the pharmaceutical *corpo técnico*, the most important members during the democratic transition period were, of the *técnicos*, Marta Nobrega Martinez, former President of CEME and currently a *técnico* with the Ministry of Science and Technology; José Scardua, former President of CEME and now working for a large bank in northeastern Brazil; Gilvan Rocha, highly nationalist President of CEME immediately after the installation of the New Republic regime; Roberto Pereira, a vice-president of CEME; Ernesto Carrera, former *técnico* at the *Conselho de Desenvolvimento Indústrial* (CDI), under the auspices of the Ministry of Industry and Commerce, who was coordinator for the original Profarma program, and now an official with the Brasilia Trade Center; and Dr Zich Moises, *técnico* in charge of the pharmaceutical sector at the Ministry of Industry and Commerce. Of the *empresários*, most important were Kurt Politzer, Executive Director of Indústrias Químicas Taubate and adviser to the democratic regime's transition team; Adilson Xavier, Executive Director of Cibran, as well as former president of Alanac; Dante Alario Junior, Executive Director of Sanus Farmacêutica, vice-president of Alanac during the New Republic era, and current president of that important lobbying organization. Of university professors, Mario Victor de Assis Pacheco was most prominent during the military regime, but continued to be a force within this segment of the *corpo técnico* after the democratic transition progressed. Especially important during the democratic transition, however, was Geraldo Giovanni, Professor of Sociology at Unicamp and a frequent panelist at conferences on the industry's prospects.

We turn, now, to presentation of individual cases from these two select groups. For the pharmaceutical *corpo técnico*, we will examine one case from each segment: i.e., a *técnico*, an *empresário*, and a university professor. Because the computer *corpo técnico* members shifted position so frequently, serving in more than one, and frequently in all three, occupational slots during the course of their careers, we will not attempt to take one member from each category. Rather, we will simply choose three of the members who were among the most relevant during the democratic transition.

Computer *Corpo Técnico*

Ivan da Costa Marques, President, Cobra

Ivan[13] had been trained as an electrical engineer at the Instituto Tecnológica da Aeronautica (ITA), a kind of Brazilian version of MIT and one of the very best of its kind in the country.[14] Upon graduation in 1967, he left to begin a doctoral program in electrical engineering at U.C. Berkeley. During the course of Ivan's stay, Berkeley, of course, was in the throes of the free speech movement and student radicalism in general.

In the midst of these events, Ivan and another Brazilian doctoral candidate and future computer *corpo técnico* member, Mario Ripper, would sometimes meet to discuss political problems at home. In Brazil, these were the years when military repression was at its most severe. Ripper and Ivan had to take care that even in far off Berkeley their discussions and actions were not somehow monitored by the dreaded *Serviço Nacional de Informações* (SNI), the Brazilian equivalent of the FBI (Dantas 1988:37). This concern in itself indicated something of the nature of these conversations. Both men opposed the military regime and were eager to see the return of democratic rule.

Upon his return to Brazil in 1972, Ivan joined the research staff at the *Nucleo de Computação Electrónico*, devoted to research in computer design, at UFRJ. After having served in this position for some time, Ivan was a logical choice to serve as head of CAPRE, the agency that served as a precursor to SEI. Later, Ivan became president of Cobra computers, the government's state enterprise in the computer industry, meant to serve as a sort of national champion in this sector.

From his base at Cobra, Ivan was able to play an important role in promoting the *corpo técnico*'s political agenda during the democratic transition. In doing this, Ivan's political characteristics came to the fore. He testified at important government hearings on the issue of political measures (financial subsidies, passage of the *Lei de Informática*, etc.), he wrote articles in favor of increased political support for the industry, and he lobbied PMDB politicians directly.

As criticism of protectionism in the computer industry mounted from other economic sectors frustrated by the relatively high cost of Brazilian computers, Ivan, along with other computer *corpo técnico* members, consistently referred to arguments that were sure to make the socially-oriented PMDB politicians see the computer *corpo técnico*'s side of the story. Such a line of argument was clearly evident by 1987, for instance, at a round-table discussion sponsored by *INFO* magazine in which Ivan participated. While acknowledging that it might seem strange to link computer industry questions with Brazil's social problems, Ivan emphasized – although in fact the link was not at all clear – that further development of the computer sector would enable Brazil to enhance the lives of its poorest citizens. The computer industry might not be as productive as some might hope, but it provided jobs, and could provide jobs for the poorest, not just the middle class ("O modelo..." 1987:9). How this would happen, however, was not really explained.

While such arguments were frequent among *corpo técnico* members at about this time, and the links between development of the computer industry and social welfare were never really clearly specified, for Ivan, at least, such statements were not mere rhetorical devices to win political support. Ivan and most of the other *corpo técnico* members, as the survey data shows, were indeed highly concerned with social issues, and Brazil's massive unemployment was one of the foremost among these. Whether increased political support for the computer industry would have a long-term impact on this problem was another question.

Edson Fregni, President, Scopus Computers

Fregni's role in supporting programs relevant to the computer industry, and his particular political characteristics, have already been discussed, to some extent, in Chapter 2. While some reiteration is inevitable, the purpose of this "representative case study" is to highlight those specific characteristics that made Fregni by far one of the most active and effective members of the computer *corpo técnico* during the democratic transition.

In terms of the three main characteristics that seemed relevant to shaping the political characteristics of *corpo técnico* members – education, age, and (for the *empresários*) nature of business ownership – Fregni clearly had all of the characteristics that set members of the computer *corpo técnico* apart from their counterparts in the pharmaceutical sector.

Fregni graduated from the University of São Paulo School of Engineering, by most rankings the finest school of its type in Brazil. Even more important than USP's and the engineering school's general reputations, however, was the fact that at the time of Fregni's studies there (late 1960s) the school was beginning its involvement in the development of Brazil's first computer. The government had selected USP to develop the prototype for one of the first Brazilian computers.

Those involved with the program, both students and professors, were an elite group, at the forefront of knowledge of electrical engineering – and certainly, computers – in the entire country. This group of students and professors, at the cutting edge of technological research in Brazil, definitely made up some of the very "best and the brightest" even within the more elite USP students.

Given the nature of this group, then, it was not all that surprising that almost every person among them later came to play an important role in the computer industry. What might have seemed surprising, however, was the extent of this group's *political* involvement in the sector. Indeed, from out of this one group came some – including Edson Fregni – who would later be among the nine or ten most politically active and involved promoters and defenders of sustained political support for the computer sector. Thus, a brief accounting of some of the activities of this group in working toward increased political support for the computer industry is instructive.

Aside from Edson Fregni himself, who went on to found the *Movimento Brasil de Informática* and became one of the most important players in this regard, there were Claudio Mammana, who, having graduated from ITA, was doing some preliminary postgraduate work before moving on to a Ph.D. program in physics at Wisconsin; and José Doria Porto, the professor in charge. All of these, Fregni included, went on to become presidents of Abicomp, the large and powerful lobbying organization for the *empresários* in the sector. Others, with lesser but still important roles, were involved in the program as well.

From these beginnings Fregni went on to do graduate work in computer science at Stanford University. Armed with his new knowledge, and already with experience in the fledgling Brazilian computer industry, Fregni went on to become a highly successful entrepreneur and founder of Scopus Computers, and probably one of the two[15] most influential, politically active, and politically "progressive" computer *corpo técnico* members during the democratic transition period. (These political characteristics served Fregni well later, when persuading the PMDB politicians to adopt a restrictive computer policy which could be seen as having a detrimental effect on economic efficiency.)

Manuel Fernando Calicchio Ruiz, President, MBI

Fernando Calicchio was a bit different from others in the computer *corpo técnico* in that he had not done graduate study in electrical engineering/computer science in the United States, and in fact held no advanced degrees in these fields. Nevertheless, Calicchio was clearly in harmony with this group both intellectually and politically.

Calicchio began his involvement with the future *corpo técnico* as early as the mid-1960s, when he studied with Milton Seligman at the Pontificia Catholic University in Rio de Janeiro (PUC/RJ). PUC/RJ – along with virtually all the institutions favored by the future computer *corpo técnico* members – was one of the best universities in Brazil. Known for its engineering department, PUC/RJ was the institution the government chose for development of the software component of the Brazilian computer industry. But Calicchio studied sociology at PUC; it was his friendship with Seligman, and a combination of other circumstances, that led to his becoming, eventually, head of the *Movimento Brasil de Informática* (MBI).

Immediately after graduating from PUC, Calicchio took a job analyzing land reform issues in Chile. This work not only contributed to the formation of Calicchio's political views about the need for land reform in Brazil, but also involved extensive use of computers. It therefore provided experience useful in a later job, working as an administrator for the Brazilian data processing association (APPD).

As mentioned in Chapter 2, the network of data processing associations (or APPDs) were significant politically in Brazil. Indeed, when the computer *corpo técnico* began making serious contacts with democratic politicians in the late 1970s, it arranged for them to address the APPD of Rio de Janeiro. Thus Calicchio was well placed to become more involved with both the industry and with the political strategies of the computer *corpo técnico*, as he did when he became head of the MBI in 1983.

With his particular political views, so much in harmony with those of his colleagues in the computer *corpo técnico* as well as with the PMDB politicians he lobbied, Calicchio was very successful in this position. Sharing their political orientation, Calicchio quickly established a rapport with key *parlamentares* in the National Congress. Indeed, he succeeded to such an extent that *deputado* and PMDB party member Antonio Gaspar, Chair of the Chamber of Deputies Commission on Science, Technology, and Informatics (the commission responsible for approving programs for the computer industry), referred to Calicchio as his "adviser" on political issues. As Gaspar explained when pressed for an interview, the researcher would do just as well in asking Calicchio about *his* views on political support for the computer industry, for anything Calicchio thought about this subject would correspond to Gaspar's own ideas![16]

In ways such as this were the computer *corpo técnico*'s various political battles won, again and again. Key PMDB politicians, trusting the computer *corpo técnico* members with whom they had such a strong political affinity, were frequently willing to go along with the *corpo técnico*'s plans for the sector wholeheartedly, despite growing evidence of some of the negative consequences (relatively high prices for domestic consumers) the market reserve law created.

Pharmaceutical *corpo técnico*

The pharmaceutical *corpo técnico*, with different political characteristics, was not as successful in obtaining favorable political outcomes (increased government support) as was the computer *corpo técnico*. The cases that follow, while not representative in each instance of the pharmaceutical *corpo técnico* as a whole, help explain – sometimes by the very factors that make them unique – why this occurred.

Roberto da Costa Pereira, Vice President, CEME

Roberto da Costa Pereira was certainly not representative. Yet examination of his case is relevant because he demonstrated how the *técnicos* in CEME, in particular, were different, politically, from other members of the pharmaceutical *corpo técnico*. Deeply concerned – as were most at CEME – with the denationalization of the pharmaceutical sector, the lack of access to medications for a large proportion of Brazil's poor, the practices of the transnational pharmaceutical firms, and the broader economic inequalities in Brazilian society as a whole, Pereira had a very favorable view of Brazil's Communist Party and voted for the Party's candidate in the first round of the 1989 elections.[17] The very fact that someone with such radical political characteristics could rise to one of the very highest positions within CEME showed that this organization was amenable to such views.

With an MBA from the University of Michigan, and a broad academic perspective on the pharmaceutical sector's prospects, Pereira had specific technical training for the kind of economic analysis he was called upon to do for CEME. As a result, he was entrusted with writing most of the text accompanying CEME's annual reports and other documents. By thus being responsible for communicating CEME's views and goals, Pereira had a great deal of influence within the organization. (He had also written a manuscript for a book, based on his historical analysis of CEME's involvement in the pharmaceutical industry.)

For instance, Roberto Pereira's views about the New Republic – and presumably CEME's views, as well – prevailed in CEME's annual reports. Pereira wrote that those working in the pharmaceutical industry had awaited the coming of the New Republic with a great deal of anticipation, and that for a time their expectations appeared to be rewarded. After the first year or so, however, the situation had reverted to what it had been before – if not worse. Before, CEME had suffered from neglect, but the *técnicos* were able to make use even of that situation, making policies of their own (such as diverting some of the operating budget for R&D) which were not strictly authorized from above, or were even illegal. Now, however, the democratically elected politicians were monitoring the industry more carefully (thus hindering such actions on the part of the CEME *técnicos*). Unfortunately, however, the new civilian politicians were not providing political support for the sector that – at least after the initially favorable prospects – was significantly any greater than what it had had before.[18]

Thus even those *técnicos* in the pharmaceutical *corpo técnico* who initially had been most favorably disposed toward the PMDB politicians were quickly disillusioned by the New Republic regime, and by the PMDB party as a whole.[19] This did not bode well for the organization's lobbying efforts, and indeed, after the very activist President, Marta Nobrega, left CEME in 1987, the organization did not constitute a strong, active lobbying presence in Brasilia.

Kurt Politzer, Executive Director, Indústrias Químicas Taubate (IQT)

Kurt Politzer represented the *empresários* segment of the pharmaceutical *corpo técnico*. Politzer's case is especially useful for depicting the general tendencies within the pharmaceutical *corpo técnico* as a whole. While not wholly representative – most *empresários*, as our survey data show, were less educated, far less active politically and, on the whole, more conservative – Politzer's views demonstrated the relatively circumscribed nature of the pharmaceutical *corpo técnico*'s political agenda.

Politzer himself was by no means politically conservative in the sense of supporting the military regime, or shunning the new democratic politicians when they came to power. For instance, after the 1985 election of Tancredo Neves, the new civilian president-elect from the PMDB party, Politzer was a key member of the transition team advising the incoming administration on industrial policy for the pharmaceutical sector. Also, Politzer was a key witness for the PMDB-dominated Senate Commission on the Pharmaceutical Industry, at which time he addressed some of the problems with denationalization the industry faced.

But Politzer never really advocated sweeping measures for reform of the sector. In 1982 he had come out in favor of some sort of market reserve, but by 1988 he had clearly modified this view.[20] By late 1989, he even seemed to be resigned to the seemingly inevitable occurrence, with the coming of the Collor Administration, of the imposition of patents of some kind in the sector.[21] Given that non-recognition of patents was the policy for which the pharmaceutical *corpo técnico* had fought hardest for years, this attitude showed how different the pharmaceutical *corpo técnico* was from the computer *corpo técnico*.

The imposition of patents for the pharmaceutical sector would not be so devastating, Politzer explained, because this would be imposition of process patents rather than product patents.[22] But what was remarkable was that given the importance he and his colleagues had placed on this issue over the years, Politzer did not seem to have any plans to fight this likely outcome at that time.[23] Certainly, there were not frequent meetings with politicians on the relevant commissions in the National Congress; nor was there a series of several public meetings throughout the country to alert the public of the pharmaceutical *corpo técnico*'s political agenda, and what it saw as the importance of the continued non-recognition of patents – all of which had happened in the computer sector.

Geraldo Giovanni, Professor, Unicamp

Geraldo Giovanni's contribution to the pharmaceutical sector was similar in some ways – but not others – to university professors in the computer industry. Trained as a sociologist at Unicamp, Giovanni wrote books documenting the problems the industry faced, and contributed editorials to newspapers in support of such programs as the Profarma. But, given the nature of the pharmaceutical industry itself, Giovanni could not bring himself to support some of the very political programs for which the rest of the pharmaceutical *corpo técnico* was working.

For instance, Giovanni was critical of Alanac, the lobbying association which, like Abicomp in the computer sector, represented the national firms for the industry. He complained that this organization represented some of the weakest of the national firms, and the reason it was so strident in its fight for non-recognition of patents was that the firms it represented would not stand much of a chance if this policy were changed. He even argued that the organization's president-elect, the director of a family-run pharmaceutical firm, was himself an inefficient manager. Such *empresários*, he claimed, sought to use government support to help them overcome their own difficulties.[24]

These views were in fact not totally valid in their sweeping criticism of Alanac members. What was remarkable about such statements, however, was that the professor who was probably the most prominent member of the "university professors" segment of the *corpo técnico* would even utter them. Prominent university professors associated with the computer industry were almost always in full agreement with the *empresários* and *técnicos* in the sector; indeed, as we have emphasized throughout, individuals within the computer *corpo técnico* often switched back and forth from one segment to another.

CONCLUSIONS

Based on the evidence, the pharmaceutical *corpo técnico* did not have young, bright, outspoken political activists fighting on its behalf to the extent that the computer *corpo técnico* did. The scarce few who did emerge came mainly from CEME, and these were not as committed to the politicians in the PMDB (as were their colleagues in the computer industry) to stick through times when the authorities were becoming discredited by the population as a whole.

Moreover, the pharmaceutical *corpo técnico* did not have widespread, strong support from local capital in the industry itself. The sort of young, highly committed and politically active individuals who were so prevalent in the private sector of the computer industry simply did not exist to any significant extent in pharmaceuticals. Where political activists from the private sector did spring up, some reputable analysts saw them as acting in a limited way on behalf of their own beleaguered firms, and not in support of broader programs to promote the national industry as a whole. At any rate, beyond attempting to prevent the institution of a law on patents – and, ultimately, failing even on that issue – they had a relatively narrow political agenda, and a political orientation different from many of the (PMDB) politicians who were in a position to help them.[25]

Largely as a consequence of such factors, the pharmaceutical *corpo técnico* had limited success in obtaining favorable political outcomes during the democratic transition period. After a brief initial increase, government political support for the pharmaceutical sector remained relatively low. Despite problems arising from the government's computer policies, support for the computer sector during this period remained relatively high and even increased. Ultimately, of course, the market reserve policy status was strengthened when it was institutionalized in the national *Lei de Informática*. Collor, despite all his efforts to eliminate the market reserve policy immediately, was forced to keep it in place longer than expected because of this earlier political triumph on the part of the computer *corpo técnico*.

5   The other variables in the model

This book seeks to explain political outcomes. Up to this point we have concentrated almost exclusively on the two clearly *political* variables in our overall model: political affinity and policy (i.e., level of government political support for given industries). In this chapter we will look more closely at the other variables in the model – in particular, "economic outcomes" – and their relationship with these political variables. For the sake of convenience, the model presented in Chapter 1 is reproduced below:

```
Foreign
ownership
and              → Access  →  Political affinity  →  Policy  →  Economic outcomes
technological
dominance
```

Figure 1   The overall model

We need to elaborate further on how how varying levels of foreign ownership and technological dominance affected the political access of the *corpos técnicos* and hence provided an opportunity for the political affinity variable to come into play. We will then turn to a discussion of how government policies in the computer and pharmaceutical industries have affected economic outcomes.

Before proceeding further, one important caveat is in order. Rather than an in-depth economic analysis, the examination here of economic outcomes will necessarily be somewhat preliminary and suggestive in nature. The focus of this book, of course, is on explaining the level of government *political* support for given industries. Moreover, it is still somewhat early to assess what the ultimate economic outcomes for the computer sector will be now that the market reserve policy has come to an end. We can, however, make a preliminary assessment.

FOREIGN OWNERSHIP AND TECHNOLOGICAL DOMINANCE

We have already discussed this variable early on in Chapter 1. A point we want to underscore here is that this variable should be seen not as an *alternative* to the political affinity explanation, but rather as a *complement* to it (as the model above illustrates). In our discussion in this chapter of the effects of policy on economic outcomes, we by no means wish to ignore or neglect the importance of economic and technological determinants; indeed, these factors are of paramount importance. For it was economic and technological factors – the level of foreign ownership and dominance of technology – that affected the extent to which the various *corpos técnicos* would be in a position to exert political influence on the government. (Political affinity would then, of course, be an additional factor that would have an effect.)

In Chapter 1, we showed that the levels of foreign ownership and technological dominance in the computer sector were low while in the pharmaceutical industry they were quite high. We argued that the varying levels of foreign ownership and technological dominance were inevitable results of the nature of the technology and the time when it was introduced.

Recent economic studies have emphasized these factors as well. The "neo-Schumpeterian" approach to industrial policy, for example, argues that technological innovations in particular industries provide a "window of opportunity" for NICs to acquire new technologies (Schmitz, Cassiolato 1992:1–20).[1] In the early phase of development of a new industry, firms from the advanced industrialized countries have not yet neccessarily been able to establish private control over the technology or a dominant position in the industry. In more mature sectors, foreign firms would already be in a position of dominance over firms in the NICs attempting to enter the sector.[2]

ACCESS

The neo-Schumpeterian view can help us to understand, then, why the level of political "access" in the Brazilian computer industry would be high when the market reserve policy was introduced, while in the pharmaceutical industry it would be low. The TNCs had not yet had time to establish a high level of foreign ownership and technological dominance in the Brazilian computer industry, or at least in the mini- and microcomputer segment of it, as they had in the pharmaceutical sector. Thus, the political room for maneuver on the part of the computer *corpo técnico* was much greater than it was for the pharmaceutical *corpo técnico*. This fact alone, however, is insufficient to explain the long tenure of the market reserve policy. Only when we combine this factor with the strong political affinity between the computer *corpo técnico* and the new dominant political elite, can we explain satisfactorily how the market reserve policy could have lasted as long as it did. The policy's endurance is especially remarkable in view of the increasingly strong economic arguments against it.

While the pharmaceutical *corpo técnico* would seem to have little opportunity to influence the government, in at least one area – where the level of foreign ownership and technological dominance was low – the pharmaceutical *corpo técnico*'s access was not limited, and there seemed to be potential for successful implementation of indstrial policies that would promote certain segments of the industry. Just as minicomputers represented one segment of the Brazilian computer market in which the government was able to act, so there was a segment of the Brazilian pharmaceutical market in which the government's actions would not have to overcome the already long-established, entrenched interests of the transnational pharmaceutical firms. This was that segment of the market represented by the Rename list.

The *Relaçâo Nacional de Medicamentos Essencias* (Rename) list was the result of CEME's long-standing proposal that the government should focus on developing a list of about 300 pharmaceutical products that were most important for the pressing needs of the Brazilian population. CEME had devised the list after its estimates indicated that, although there were over 4,000 different pharmaceutical products on the Brazilian market – many of them representing only different foreign brand names – the 300 or so products on the Rename list would serve about 90 percent of the basic needs of the Brazilian population. As noted, the Rename list was a specific market niche that the TNCs had not yet come to dominate. The transnationals had chosen not to develop many of the Rename products in Brazil either because these products were less profitable than others, or because they were not suited to the needs of the markets in the developed nations, and producing them only for the Brazilian market would be too difficult.[3]

Thus, even in the pharmaceutical industry there did appear to be some room for the government to operate and maneuver (a high degree of "access"). Increased government political support for the sector – at least for a specialized segment of the market – *was* possible, at least as possible, arguably, as it was for a specialized segment of the computer sector. But lack of broad government policies for CEME, as well as for the development of crucial *matérias-primas*, or primary ingredients, kept government political support for the sector low.

MEASURES OF THE EFFECTS ON ECONOMIC OUTCOMES OF KEY GOVERNMENT POLICIES

Having considered the varying extent to which economic and technological constraints limited the government's ability to implement effective industrial

policies, we can now examine the effects on economic outcomes of government policies that *were* implemented. In order to assess economic outcomes,
we need to consider such factors as profits and the level of national ownership, the development of indigenous technological capability (especially as
measured by development of human resources), and the kinds of products the
companies were selling (and to whom). Because developments and trends in
the two sectors were somewhat different, we will focus on certain aspects of
the economic outcomes in the computer sector (specifically, the relative
prices for Brazilian computer products relative to foreign firms, and the
"disarticulation" of policy in the sector) that we will not address in the
pharmaceutical sector. Similarly, we will devote particular attention to an
economic phenomenon ("denationalization") in the pharmaceutical industry
which did not occur in the computer sector.

Of all the factors that we will examine, development of indigenous
technological capability (especially human resources) deserves special emphasis. In NICs seeking to improve their economic status *vis-à-vis* the
advanced industrialized nations, development of indigenous technological
capability is an important aspect of an effective industrial policy. Indeed,
development of such capability is crucial if industrialization is to bring about
sustainable economic growth (Dietz 1990:178).

In Chapter 1 we referred to Sanjaya Lall's useful definition of "national
technological capabilities," which consists of three components: physical
investment (plant and equipment as well as financial resources), human
capital (skills), and technological effort ("efforts by productive enterprises to
assimilate and improve upon the relevant technology") (Lall 1992). Other
definitions of indigenous or national technological capabilities consistently
mention similar components (Enos 1991:12). All include what would appear
to be an essential ingredient of indigenous technological capability, the
development of human resources and skills. In assessing the economic effects
of government policies, then, we need to pay special attention to this factor.

National ownership and production is an important part of the development of human resources. In the Brazilian computer industry, for example,
Schmitz and Hewitt note that "it is beyond doubt that the national computer
firms employ more of their human resources in R&D than foreign firms do"
(Schmitz, Hewitt 1992:36). Indeed, these authors found that foreign firms
employ only 3.7 percent of their employees in R&D, as opposed to 12.5
percent for national firms (Schmitz, Hewitt 1992:35). Thus, different levels
of national ownership for the two industries will serve as one rough indicator
for economic "success," as will the other factors, such as profits and relative
prices, that we mentioned above.

EFFECTS OF GOVERNMENT POLICIES ON ECONOMIC OUTCOMES IN THE COMPUTER AND PHARMACEUTICAL INDUSTRIES

Several government policies in particular stand out as having helped shape economic developments in the two industries. For the computer industry, the key policy, of course, was the market reserve. For the pharmaceutical sector, key policies were SUMOC 113 of the late 1950s and early 1960s (explained in detail below); the lack of strong political support for CEME and Profarma; and, most recently, various smaller projects supported with funding from some state agencies. We will assess each industry in turn.

The computer industry

For the computer industry, the market reserve policy had some negative consequences, but when analyzed in terms of this one industry itself, the effects – at least up until the late 1980s – would have to be judged as predominantly positive.

Positive effects

In 1991, the National Congress took steps to relax the market reserve. By 1992, it had been eliminated altogether, although tariffs remained as high as 40 percent. A certain number of Brazilian computer firms were likely to be eliminated under the new arrangements. Nevertheless, by this time the market reserve had given national firms the opportunity to develop sufficient indigenous technological capabilities – in particular, a base of highly trained technicians and engineers – to enable them to negotiate with foreign firms on the terms of joint venture agreements. As Schmitz and Cassiolato note, "The clearest indication of the growing capacity of both industry and government in Brazil is the turnaround in the willingness of foreign capital to negotiate over technology transfer to local firms" (Schmitz, Cassiolato 1992:16). In this regard, then, as well as in the development of at least some Brazilian-designed products – e.g., banking automation systems – the market reserve policy had resulted in successful, enduring outcomes for the Brazilian computer industry.

The market reserve had to be altered because by the mid-1980s, many Brazilian computer users – industrial, military, and otherwise – were beginning to complain about the restrictiveness of the policy. (We will assess these criticisms more explicitly in the section on "Negative Effects," below.) Despite this political opposition, however, the government's computer policy, in the relatively short time of its existence, was remarkably successful as measured in terms of national ownership and profits and the development of indigenous technological capabilities.

National ownership and profits

In 1970, before the market reserve policy was put into effect, virtually all computers in Brazil were made by the TNCs. By the late 1980s, Brazil had developed the largest national computer industry in the Third World. Under the protection of the market reserve policy, the number of domestic companies operating in the sector rose from 29 (75 percent of the total) in 1980, to 310 (90 percent of the total) in 1986 (Latin American Development Bank 1988:138). By the late 1980s total profits for the sector as a whole, both foreign and domestic firms, were on the order of 4 billion. From 1979 to 1986, gross profits for domestic firms alone in the sector increased from $190 million to $1.53 billion, a 705 percent increase in current values. Although transnational corporations operated in a separate segment of the market, profits for these firms increased also, but by a smaller amount – from $640 million to $1.47 billion – a 130 percent increase in current values (Latin American Development Bank 1988:137).

In 1979, just two years after the government had established the market reserve, gross profits in the Brazilian computer industry were $830 million, of which 77 percent still went to foreign firms, and only 23 percent to national companies. By 1988, gross profits had grown to $4.428 billion, of which only 33 percent went to foreign firms (producing primarily large computers, such as mainframes, not included in the market reserve) and 67 percent went to national companies (Abicomp 1989).

As the above data indicate, foreign firms still continued to participate in the Brazilian computer market after the establishment of the market reserve in 1977. But because the highly dynamic mini- and microcomputer market was protected, foreign firms supplied the much smaller segment of the market consisting of mainframes and larger computers. Of the 723,000 computers in Brazil in 1987, national firms had manufactured 97 percent (Abicomp 1989:6). (Of course, these larger and more complex computers tended to be much more expensive than their smaller counterparts; one source estimated that, on the average, each of the foreign computers was worth as much as 50 times more than the types Brazilian firms manufactured (Abicomp 1989).

Development of indigenous technological capability

Even beyond the dramatic transformation in ownership and profits, Brazil, with the market reserve policy, had achieved what many "dependency" theorists had argued that it could never do, i.e., develop indigenous technological capabilities in a high-technology industry. Even Peter Evans, whose earlier theories had discounted the possibility of Brazil's accomplishing such a feat, had to admit this. Acknowledging Brazil's successes with the industry as a result of the market reserve policy, Evans pointed out that, "most impressive of all," Brazil had "generated local capacity for product innovation" (Evans 1986:800). This was precisely what Evans's earlier work, *Dependence and Development*, had explained would not be possible in Brazil (Evans 1979).

One area in which the Brazilian computer firms were especially innovative was in automation of banking services. Beginning in the late 1960s, the Brazilian government, seeking to promote efficiency in the huge country's financial system, pushed for the centralization and concentration of Brazil's many regional banks. Unimpeded by anti-trust legislation, Brazilian banks consolidated, growing in size and diminishing in number. Today, "five of the ten largest banks in Latin America (in terms of stock-holding equity) are Brazilian" (Cassiolato 1992:61).

Because of this unique concentration of the financial system in Brazil, banks were forced to seek out – and in some cases, develop on their own – innovative data processing strategies and products. As a result, Brazilian banks became some of the principal consumers (and in some cases, producers) of Brazilian-designed computer products. For example, the new national Brazilian banks, no longer able to rely on data-processing centers to process documents overnight and return them to various branches scattered throughout the country the next day, were forced to develop their own kind of minicomputers for each bank branch that were specifically tailored to this need. One bank, Bradesco, went so far as to create its own automation technology laboratory. An important innovation to come out of this effort – as early as 1978 – was the first system ever developed for machine-read magnetic characters that could be printed on checks and processed by automatic teller machines (Cassiolato 1992:61).

In addition to these direct technological developments, the large number of national computer firms promoted the development of human resources and capital. Significantly, the national firms employed far more Brazilians than the foreign firms: in 1988, 54,714 Brazilians worked for national firms, as opposed to only 13,550 for foreign companies (Abicomp 1989).

Of course, a high rate of employment might mean only that the industry was inefficient and unproductive. As indicated earlier, however, the percentage of the workforce these firms employed in R&D was very high, at 12.5 percent. One study found that foreign firms tended to employ engineers in activities such as marketing and management rather than R&D (Hewitt 1992:193). This evidence confirms the complaints of newly-minted Brazilian Ph.D.s in electrical engineering and computer science in the late 1960s, before a national computer industry had been established. Upon returning to Brazil, these highly trained individuals found their opportunities limited to such activities as working as salesmen for IBM. Indeed, as Adler (Adler 1987) has pointed out, it was in part the frustration of these future *corpo técnico* members that helped spark the drive for a national computer industry in Brazil. They knew that in their own national firms, their skills and talents would be more productively employed.

Negative effects

Of course, some negative consequences of the policy did exist, and their effects increased over time. These resulted in part from the inherent problems associated with protectionism for an emerging industry.

Relative prices, quality, and competitiveness

For one thing, the market reserve had stimulated the emergence of a great number of new domestic firms. This had positive aspects in terms of the development of human resources, and it did spur internal competition among firms behind the protectionist barriers (Schmitz, Hewitt 1992:27). Nevertheless, many of the firms created during the market reserve years were doomed quickly to go defunct without the buffer from international competition the policy provided; and indeed, with the elimination of major elements of the market reserve in 1991, this is precisely what began to happen.

The reason for this was that the national firms lacked competitiveness with the foreign firms in terms of price and quality. Continuous reductions in prices for foreign computers meant constant increases in relative prices for Brazilian computers, especially PC-compatible microcomputers, one of the main products of the Brazilian industry. Prices for peripheral computer products remained at a level two to four times higher than that for the same kinds of products on the US market (Tigre 1988:63). For Brazilian computer products in general, prices were roughly twice those of prices for the equivalent products in the United States (Schmitz, Hewitt 1992:28). The only Brazilian-made computer products that were cheaper than those available on world markets were those related to banking automation systems (Schmitz, Hewitt 1992:31). With regard to quality, Brazilian banking automation systems again stood out; these were, in fact, exported to other Latin American countries and to Europe. But in other areas, Brazilian computer products tended generally to be about two years behind the latest state-of-the-art technology available on world markets (Schmitz, Hewitt 1992:31).

"Disarticulation" of policy

Thus, the relatively high prices and poor quality for the sector's products in Brazil, in comparison with what was available on world markets, were still a serious concern for the industry in the early 1990s.[4] Such difficulties were the legacy of more serious structural problems, resulting from the lack of policy coordination – even when the market reserve policy was still in full force – among different parts of the Brazilian "electronics complex." The electronics complex encompassed three sectors: computers, telecommunications, and consumer electronics. Unlike the case in a country such as South Korea, in which large, single firms might engage in manufacturing activities encompassing all of these sectors, in Brazil these activities were separate, and the sectors remained quite distinct from one another. Government policy was similarly distinct and separate toward each of these sectors.

As many computer *corpo técnico* members frequently pointed out, this "disarticulation" of government policy toward the three sectors prevented Brazilian firms from obtaining economies of scale, an important objective to meet if Brazilian computer firms were to improve the quality of their products and bring down prices.[5] Accomplishing these goals was essential if Brazilian firms were going to attempt to compete with products available on the international market. After the elimination of the market reserve in 1992, some sort of increased coordination toward the three sectors – still not fully achieved – became all the more necessary.

The main obstacle to the coordination of the three sectors was that because they had evolved at different times and under different sets of circumstances, each one of them came under the administrative authority of different government agencies. These agencies had widely divergent policy agendas. For example, the Ministry of Science and Technology, responsible for the computer industry, wanted to increase the technological capabilities of key Brazilian industries. In the years immediately before the elimination of the market reserve policy in 1992, it fought hard to preserve – and, beyond that, extend – the market reserve. The Ministry of Communications (Minicom), on the other hand, was more concerned with ensuring that Brazil had high-quality, relatively inexpensive (in effect, *foreign*) communications technology. Thus, Minicom was often in conflict with the Ministry of Science and Technology and members of the computer *corpo técnico* over this issue.

The inter-governmental conflicts did not end there. The Ministry of Science and Technology was also at odds with the Superintendency of the Free Zone of Manaus (Surframa), which administered a tariff-free zone in Manaus, a city in the impoverished northern state of Amazonas. Set up in the late 1960s as a means of attracting foreign investment (and jobs) to an underdeveloped region of Brazil, Manaus' free trade zone had become a center for foreign imports of consumer electronics goods. While the substantial tax concessions the government granted to foreign firms which set up manufacturing operations in the Zone, along with the less rigid requirements on percentage of nationally manufactured components used, did encourage foreign companies to locate in the region, the result was that Brazilian consumer electronics firms were unable to compete. Consequently, Brazilian efforts to develop indigenous technological capabilities in this sector were virtually eliminated. As Tigre notes, the result was the "complete denationalization" of radio and television manufacturing (consumer electronics) in Brazil in the 1960s (Tigre 1987:81).

Fearing a similar fate, members of the computer *corpo técnico* fought to have the provisions of the protectionist computer market reserve apply even in the Free Zone of Manaus. This set off a political battle between the computer *corpo técnico* and Surframa during the national debate over the provisions of the *Lei de Informática*. Using their political affinity with the ruling PMDB politicians, members of the computer *corpo técnico* managed to obtain a favorable outcome, although more limited than that for which they had hoped: the government would restrict the *amount* of benefits going to those computer firms that sought to locate their operations in the Free Zone (Tigre 1987:81).

While the computer *corpo técnico* was (relatively) victorious in this instance, the fundamental structural problems remained. In all, however, the computer industry's difficulties were minor in comparison with the pharmaceutical industry's problems. The Brazilian computer industry had, by 1992, managed to develop sufficient indigenous technological capabilities so that at least some of its larger and more successful firms would be able to survive. The government's policies had to be considered successful in the sense that a local computer industry – including a well-developed base of human capital and considerable indigenous technological capability in certain areas, for example, banking automation systems – had come into existence (and seemed likely to continue to exist) where virtually nothing had existed before.

The pharmaceutical industry

Notwithstanding the (relatively) minor complaints from domestic consumers about the computer industry, economic outcomes in the pharmaceutical industry were much less favorable. By far the most distinctive aspect of this industry, very much in contrast to the computer sector, was "denationalization." This was the gradual *loss* of national ownership over time as the transnational corporations, with superior technology, increasingly dominated this sector.

A number of factors explain why economic outcomes for the two industries diverged so greatly. Among these are the technological factors discussed in Chapter 1. But a government policy known as SUMOC 113[6] (a law promoting virtually unrestricted foreign investment in the sector), as well as the government's failure to provide strong support for CEME and for the Profarma proposal, were important factors contributing to this result. Even as these high-level policy débâcles were occurring, however, middle-level *técnicos* working within state agencies such as CEME (and elsewhere), were taking action. These *técnicos* planned and implemented policies that demonstrated not only that significant government political support for the pharmaceutical sector was possible, but that such policies could make a difference in economic outcomes for the industry.

Because denationalization was so significant in this sector, an assessment of economic outcomes in the pharmaceutical industry requires a detailed discussion of this phenomenon, and of SUMOC 113's role in creating it. Accordingly, in our assessment of this sector we will take an approach that differs somewhat from the one we used for the computer industry. Here, we will first discuss briefly discuss some of the factors relevant to our measures of economic outcomes. But since the denationalization phenomenon is so significant for this industry, we will then turn to a detailed discussion of that phenomenon itself. After that, we can examine some of the later efforts, on the part of some of the *técnicos*, which produced both frustrating and positive results.

National ownership and profits

By the late 1980s, Brazil represented the seventh largest pharmaceutical market in the world, with transactions amounting to approximately $1.9 billion per year. Yet this market was dominated by transnational corporations. Of approximately 470 pharmaceutical firms operating in Brazil, about 390 were either Brazilian-owned or joint ventures with partly Brazilian capital (Gerez, Pedrosa 1987:15). But just 80 TNCs dominated 83 percent of the market, while the 15 biggest national firms controlled only 11 percent (Viegas 1987:5). Because of the massive denationalization that had taken place in the sector in previous decades, by 1985 no domestic firms were among the top 20 pharmaceutical firms in the Brazilian market; in fact, they controlled only 17 percent of the market in the country as a whole (Gerez, Pedrosa 1987:15).

Development of indigenous technological capability

In the production of *fármacos*, the raw materials or primary ingredients from which medications were made – the most highly advanced phase of pharmaceutical manufacture – the transnationals had a clear superiority over the Brazilian firms. Firms with predominantly national capital produced only about 22 percent of these crucial ingredients, while firms with predominantly foreign capital produced 78 percent (Ferraz 1988:11). Moreover, as we documented in Chapter 3, those working in this industry – unlike their counterparts in the computer industry – were far less likely to have advanced technical training.

Denationalization

In order to understand these specific economic outcomes, we need to understand the larger phenomenon of the denationalization of the pharmaceutical industry. Because the denationalization process occurred gradually, over the course of many years, an appreciation of the extent of this phenomenon requires some historical context.

Unlike the computer industry, which was just beginning to develop in Brazil in the late 1960s and early 1970s, the pharmaceutical industry had a long tradition in Brazil. In fact, by the late 1800s, it had become a thriving economic sector – albeit one that was very different from the kind of pharmaceutical industry existing in Brazil today.

In the late 1800s, the pharmaceutical industry was actually a largely Brazilian-owned sector that made products such as elixirs and salves. The industry, as Evans has noted, was similar in many ways to the pharmaceutical industry in the United States at the time, and had similarly high levels of national ownership (Evans 1979:9).

The technological advances in antibiotics developed to treat wounded soldiers in World War II, however, set off a process of technological development in the pharmaceutical industry that left Brazil far behind. With their superior technological know-how, firms from the industrialized countries quickly came to dominate world markets with their new, powerful drugs. As profits grew, these firms were able to invest even more capital in research and development, as well as in marketing. Over time, as the Brazilian pharmaceutical firms became increasingly less competitive, their market shares and profits dwindled. Eventually, firms that often had been owned by a single family for decades had to be sold.

Recent data (see Table 5.1) shows how the trend has continued since the 1950s:

.

Table 5.1   National firms among 20 largest in market

Year	No. of firms	Firms
1957	5	Pinheiros, Moura Brasil, Torres, Inst. Med. Foura, Lafi
1960	4	Pinheiros, Torres, Lafi, Inst. Med. Foura
1962	4	Pinheiros, Inst. Med. Foura, Lafi, Torres
1972	—	—
1975	1	Ache
1985	—	—
1990	—	—

Source: Presented in Gerez, Pedroza 1987: 15; and current documents

Eventually, then, and at an accelerating pace in the 1960s and 1970s, this process of denationalization and loss of market share reached devastating proportions. And all of this occurred at the same time that the Brazilian pharmaceutical market, as a by-product of the rapid (but highly inegalitarian) economic growth of the 1960s and 1970s, had become the seventh largest in the world.[7]

Many analysts argued that, given the structure of the Brazilian pharmaceutical industry, there was virtually nothing that could be done to reverse this situation. As Chapter 3 has shown, the foreign pharmaceutical firms maintained what appeared to be almost a vise-like grip on the making of policy for the sector. The entrenched interests of the transnational pharmaceutical firms were simply too strong to be overcome. Even when assorted *técnicos* in CEME, for instance, did attempt to support broad policy initiatives to restructure the industry, other elements within the government fought against the changes. The sector seemed clearly to support Evans's arguments about high-technology industries in the NICs being unable to overcome such obstacles.

That interpretation was at least open for debate, as we will show below. But as a kind of foreshadowing of our ultimate argument – that government policies could indeed make some difference and that lack of government political support had political as well as economic causes – we will first show how some very bad policy, specifically, SUMOC 113, and later, the events related to CEME and the Profarma proposal, accelerated the negative outcomes that were occurring in this sector. Then we will go on to show that with certain helpful policies some positive results could, in fact, occur.

SUMOC 113, a policy of the Kubitschek Administration, was one of the immediate causes of the massive denationalization that occurred in the 1960s.

A complicated bit of legislation involving foreign exchange rates,[8] it greatly facilitated foreign investment in the Brazilian pharmaceutical industry. By making it more profitable for the foreign firms to invest in Brazil, the Kubitschek Administration hoped to increase the rate of foreign investment in the country. Doing this, economic theoreticians and policymakers of the day believed, would enable Brazil to develop quickly, even to attain, as the Kubitschek slogan went, "fifty years of development in five."

Ideas such as these, known as "developmentalism," pervaded the consciousness of those who made and thought about public policy in Brazil in the 1950s and 1960s. Significantly, the Kubitscheck era was the zenith of developmentalism in Brazil. The problem with this approach, however, was that foreign investment sometimes, to use the technical economic term, "crowded out" domestic investment. If the transnational corporations already had a technological advantage in a particular industry, then with still more financial incentives to invest in Brazil they would develop virtually a stranglehold on the Brazilian market. Brazilian firms, unable to compete, would find themselves "crowded out" of the market, and denationalization of the industry would occur.

Of course, the argument of Peter Evans's "triple alliance" approach, as presented in his 1979 book *Dependent Development*, was that Brazilian (or Mexican, or Nigerian) firms could still find an economic niche, and benefit from economic growth, even if they did not have the same technological capabilities of the transnational firms. The local companies could form joint ventures with the foreign firms (often with the state making up the third part of the "triple alliance" of investors), and fill crucial roles where they had special expertise – for instance, in marketing (Evans 1979).

Evans, of course, argued that domestic firms in high technology industries would *not* be able simply to catch up with the foreign firms by developing technology of their own. Instead, they would have to be mere beneficiaries of foreign firms, for the transnational corporations possessed the driving force – technology – that kept the whole capitalist process in motion. Thus, the development that took place as a result of these triple alliance arrangements was still *dependent* development.

With policies such as SUMOC 113 to assist the process, the *dependent* character of this dependent development was bound to increase over time, as Table 5.1 above demonstrates that it certainly did in the pharmaceutical industry. Lack of political support for CEME and for policies such as the Profarma proposal, as documented in Chapter 3, did nothing to improve the situation. Of course, some might argue that the economic situation in the industry had already reached the state at which supporting CEME and Profarma not only would have been impossible politically but would have been useless economically as well. But other activities were taking place within the sector, less controversial and less publicized than these, that indicate that positive change within the sector was possible.

Efforts by the técnicos

As noted in Chapter 3, even after its administrative restructuring, CEME continued (clandestinely, yet!) to channel 5 percent of its operating budget into research and development. Much of this money went to fund the *Companhia de Desenvolvimento Tecnológico* (Codotec), a national firm that provided services to Brazilian companies trying to develop domestic technology. Founded in 1976, Codotec was a creation of the *Universidade Estadual de Campinas* (Unicamp), one of Brazil's best universities for scientific research, and the *Secretaria de Tecnológia Industrial* (STI). The head of the STI at that time happened to be José Walter Bautista Vidal, a highly nationalist *técnico* (a fact that probably helped in getting the project under way). Codotec functioned as an R&D and consulting agency devoted to technological matters. National firms would form contracts with researchers at Codotec to develop specific products, and Codotec, exemplifying the crucial linkage between university and industry that had always been so important in the development of North American high-tech industries, would take advantage of its numerous Unicamp-trained and/or affiliated researchers to fill the contract.

In 1983, the same year that it became officially independent of Unicamp, Codotec began to work with *química fina*, as the chemical-pharmaceutical sector was called in Brazil. The impetus for this involvement came from CEME, which was determined to develop Brazil's technological capabilities in the chemical-pharmaceutical area. In providing funding for Codotec's activities in this sector, CEME hoped to create a research team capable of technological and scientific support for Brazilian firms. The ultimate goal was to overturn Brazil's great dependence on foreign technology for the manufacture of *fármacos* or *matérias-primas*, the raw materials from which finished pharmaceutical products were made.[9] As noted, these materials, which required advanced chemical manufacturing processes to produce, were the stage of the industry that required the most sophisticated technological ability.

A number of important Brazilian firms were able, with the assistance of Codotec, to develop substantial technology for the manufacture of pharmaceutical products. Specifically, the services Codotec provided to these firms were "development of production processes, absorption of technology acquired abroad, and technical assistance in the establishment of industrial production of raw materials" (Rimoli 1987:9). For instance, Rimoli cites the example of the *Laboratório Industrial Brasileiro de Biologia e Síntese*

(Libbs). Because of its lack of specialized personnel, Libbs was having trouble getting started with the difficult raw materials production phase. With financial assistance from the STI, Libbs was able to obtain Codotec's services to develop production processes. The final result was that Libbs was able to develop at least one medication that could be used to substitute imported versions of the same product (Rimoli 1987:9–10).

Other national efforts continued as well, despite the weakening of CEME and the lack of support for the Profarma plan. Several firms continued to attempt to develop *matérias-primas*, some working with Codotec on these endeavors. Other firms received assistance directly from government agencies such as CEME, the Ministry of Science and Technology,[10] and the *Financiadora de Projetos* (Finep), under the auspices of the *Banco Nacional de Desenvolvimento Econômico* (BNDE). Thus, as a result of actions by concerned *técnicos* within these agencies, government support for some individual projects and individual firms continued to go forward quietly and without controversy. Still another occurrence along these same lines was that various pharmaceutical research institutes, including the two most renowned in Brazil – *Fundação Instituto Oswaldo Cruz* (Fiocruz) and *Instituto Butantan* – signed agreements with CEME to develop projects designed to overcome Brazil's dependence on antibiotic serums and vaccines.

Still other individual efforts at import substitution of *matérias-primas* continued among prominent Brazilian firms with a majority of national capital. CEME provided indirect (and again, uncontested) support for many of these efforts by means of its still-remaining "power of the purchase." That is, the agency bought as many products as possible, of those that were on the Rename list, from national firms.

Benefitting from such support, some Brazilian firms were able to develop successful – and profitable – projects. For instance, the *Companhia Brasileira de Antibióticos* (Cibran),[11] managed to develop three *fármacos* used in making medications for pneumonia, urinary infections, and respiratory illnesses, that saved Brazil millions of dollars in imports. Manufacturing the *fármaco* known as *lincomicina*, used in creating medications for treatment of pneumonia, saved Brazil $10 million dollars per year alone (Rimoli 1987:10). Another saving was made on Brazil's ever-strained foreign exchange reserves came when *Carbonatos do Nordeste* S/A (Carbonor) began producing bicarbonite of soda in 1983. Because of this product's many uses in pharmaceutical manufacturing, Brazil had been spending $6 million dollars in importing it every year. After Carbonor began operations, however, Brazil was quickly relieved of dependence on this substance, and by 1987, Carbonor was actually exporting it and bringing *in* foreign exchange (Rimoli 1987:11). Another example of this kind of positive result took place in that same year, when two firms under the administration of Kurt Politzer – an important *corpo técnico* member mentioned in Chapter 3 – were beginning to enjoy similarly spectacular success. *Indústrias Químicas Taubate* (IQT), of which Politzer was President, and *Guanabara Técnica e Industrial S/A* (Getec), saved in the range of $27 million dollars in 1987 by using their own *farmacos* in producing a number of finished medications (Rimoli 1987:13).

Thus, government support for programs and projects to develop domestic technological capabilities in the pharmaceutical sector *was* feasible, and it *could* produce significant economic results. As José Carlos Campana Gerez, Director of R&D for Codotec, said: "it's possible to grow and invest in this sector, to the contrary of what the multinationals proclaim" (Rimoli 1987:9). What was needed was government political support which, while avoiding the opposition of the transnationals, still managed to produce positive economic results. The efforts made in that direction described above indicated that such support was possible.

CONCLUSIONS

Having assessed economic outcomes, we can now draw some general conclusions. One is that the Brazilian computer industry benefitted from timing (as we will explain more fully in a moment). Another is that the pharmaceutical industry, despite (by the 1980s) the clear technological and economic obstacles to attaining favorable political – as well as economic – outcomes, *could* move in the direction of attaining those outcomes when certain political conditions were met.

The computer industry benefitted from timing partly because, unlike the case with the pharmaceutical industry in the 1950s and early 1960s, those responsible for the making of policy understood the importance of providing measures to protect infant industries. The old "developmentalist" ideas of the 1950s and early 1960s had been surpassed, by this time, by the "dependency" concepts Latin American economists had developed earlier. If policymakers for the pharmaceutical industry had understood the problems inherent in unrestricted promotion of massive foreign investment earlier, such damaging policies as SUMOC 113 might never have been instituted.

The other way in which the timing factor gave the computer industry an advantage over the pharmaceutical industry – as already noted briefly in Chapter 1 – was that foreign computer firms had not yet established a strong foothold in the Brazilian computer sector when the market reserve policy was put in place. In the pharmaceutical industry, in contrast, as events amply demonstrated, political opposition from long-established TNCs was often overpowering. By the time new approaches to industrial development had become more widely accepted, the TNCs had already acquired a firm foothold in the market. Major policy initiatives that would have advanced technological development in the sector in a significant way, e.g., the strengthening of CEME or the Profarma, were, in effect, vetoed by the overwhelming political force of the foreign interests.

Mention of the failure of these two particular policies leads us to a second observation, one that provides some basis for hope for the ultimate fate of the Brazilian pharmaceutical industry. The development of the (originally) powerful CEME, and the Profarma proposal, were very broad, all-encompassing, highly publicized policies that sought – or at least had the potential – to bring about wide-ranging, radical change for the sector. The grand scale of these policies, their potentially widespread effects on the sector as a whole, and the resultant publicity they generated, were some of the very factors that made them so controversial politically. Such policies were quick to draw vehement protests from the politically powerful TNCs.

Other policies, however, such as CEME's funnelling of 5 percent of its annual operating budget to R&D, and the combined support of Finep and the Ministry of Science and Technology for relatively unpublicized, individual projects of relatively small scale, were much more successful. Because such policies did not attract as much attention as broader, all-encompassing policy initiatives such as CEME and Profarma, they were far less controversial and did not provoke strong political opposition on the part of the TNCs. Thus, in the Brazilian pharmaceutical sector, "muddling through"[12] with smaller, individual efforts seemed to be the approach to policymaking most likely to produce results.

6 Application of the argument to other cases

While the argument advanced here is valid for the cases examined thus far, the real test is to apply it to other cases. In this chapter, then, we will analyze to what extent our main hypothesis (in comparison with some alternatives) applies to the nuclear power industry in Brazil, Argentina, and South Korea. While testing the hypothesis with reference to the computer and pharmaceutical industries in Argentina and South Korea might have provided a useful comparative perspective, sufficient secondary data on the political affinity variable for these two industries – in these as well as in other NICs – is simply not available.

The nuclear sector is particularly relevant to this study because, like those sectors examined in the primary cases, it is a high-technology industry.[1] The nuclear industry is especially appropriate for our analysis of political affinity, as well, because – even more so than the computer industry – the nuclear sector is also a security-related industry. Development of nuclear power technology almost inevitably goes hand in hand with development of the potential to make nuclear weapons.

For the nuclear cases, as with the primary ones (Brazilian computer and pharmaceutical industries), certain key variables were especially important in determining political outcomes. But in the nuclear cases, the key variables operated in ways that were more complicated than in the primary cases. For instance, the degree of access *usually* determined the extent of influence the political affinity variable could have. In some instances, however, a low degree of access seemed even to increase the influence of the political affinity variable. The case studies explain and elaborate on these different ways in which the key variables functioned.

The nuclear cases are unique in that, in addition to the access and political affinity variables, a distinctive combination of international prestige and national security concerns also had influence on government political support for the sector. The NIC military governments perceived the prestige component of national security to be very important, for in their view a nation's possession of nuclear capability – even if it were merely a few nuclear power plants – conferred a certain status of having entered "the nuclear age." And of course, with nuclear power plants and associated technology came the capability (at more advanced technological levels) to manufacture materials, such as enriched uranium and plutonium, which were crucial ingredients in the construction of nuclear weapons. As we will see, this strong association between the nuclear industry and military concerns had an effect on the political affinity variable.

In broad terms, political affinity is the extent of similarity between the political characteristics of a given industry's *corpo técnico* and a dominant political coalition or party. As explained in Chapter 1, this variable has two components. One aspect of political affinity is the ability of the *corpo técnico* to influence government policies. Another aspect is the degree of willingness and enthusiasm of the *corpo técnico* members to promote and work on particular industrial programs that are seen as serving the interests of the dominant coalition or party. In the cases to be examined here,[2] one or the other (or both) aspects of the political affinity variable were significant in determining outcomes.

All of the countries examined here are newly industrializing countries[3] that have either undergone or are in the process of undergoing "democratization." Indeed, the prevalence of this trend toward democratization among NICs worldwide makes the present analysis particularly relevant. Because of the importance of this phenomenon for the cases to be discussed here and for the overall analysis, we must mention briefly the specific ways in which it has occurred in Argentina and South Korea.

Argentina underwent a transition to civilian rule after the military's defeat in the Falklands war of 1982. Although the consolidation of civilian rule has been threatened at times by the severe economic crisis the country is experiencing, civilian rule has prevailed since that time. While policymaking in South Korea remains authoritarian in many respects, South Korea, too, has experienced a democratic transition. The consolidation of full-fledged democracy in South Korea is, in fact, an ongoing process that began in 1987. In each of these instances of transition, the extent of the movement toward greater democratization, itself one of the elements making up the political affinity variable, helped shape how this variable influenced outcomes. Using this variable, then, the cases explain why government political support for the nuclear sector remained high in Argentina and South Korea, but declined significantly in Brazil.

"ACCESS" AND THE NUCLEAR INDUSTRY

Before proceeding to the individual country cases, we must discuss briefly the influence of the access variable in this sector. Then we can go on to show how access affected political affinity.

Immediately after World War II, the United States clearly dominated the nuclear industry both technologically and economically. Only a few other nations (Great Britain, France, and the Soviet Union) possessed nuclear technology of any kind at this time. While widespread development of nuclear technology, including production of nuclear weapons, appeared to be something that could happen only in the distant future, it seemed likely that nuclear technology would spread to many other countries, even Third World countries, over time. Indeed, as early as 1954, Indian scientists were designing their own nuclear research reactor (Subramanian, Mohan 1982:167).

In response to what seemed to be the inevitable diffusion of nuclear technology, the Eisenhower Administration began a program known as "Atoms for Peace." The idea behind the program was that if other nations could not be stopped in their efforts to acquire nuclear technology, then at least the United States should try to guide them toward its peaceful uses. The way to do this, the US policymakers believed, was to provide nuclear technology to other countries on the condition that it not be used for military purposes. In addition, recipient nations would have to adhere to certain safeguards and permit the International Atomic Energy Agency (IAEA) to make inspections to ensure that the conditions were being met.

A major flaw with this policy, however, was that it did not explicitly forbid recipient nations from developing nuclear weapons on their own, or prevent them from acquiring the requisite technology from other nations. Crucial to the manufacture of such weapons was the ability to "enrich," or reprocess, the uranium fuels that nuclear power stations used in producing electricity. The United States government refused to export this technology; yet, since at that time the US sold only light water reactors (LWRs) which required enriched uranium to function, purchasers of these reactors were dependent on the United States for a steady supply of enriched uranium fuel. Under such circumstances, the NICs had motivation to acquire the technology for the entire nuclear fuel cycle, including the capability to enrich uranium.

As the United States gradually lost its monopoly on nuclear technology, it came to lose its monopolistic control over the market for this technology as well. This development facilitated domestic control and access over policymaking for the nuclear industry in the NICs. With more opportunities to bargain with increasing numbers of "nuclear" nations for a greater transfer of technology, policymakers in the NICs could request more favorable terms in contracts to build nuclear power plants. Now they could demand transfer of the entire nuclear fuel cycle – including the reprocessing, "enrichment" phase which the United States had refused to provide.

Thus, the access variable did not present an obstacle to policymaking in the nuclear sector. NIC policymakers were not necessarily predisposed to oppose high levels of government support for indigenous development in the nuclear industry. In this sector, therefore, the influence of other variables – political affinity and policymakers' concerns about prestige and national security – took on special importance in determining outcomes. Accordingly, these variables, and particularly the political affinity variable, are the focus of the cases below.

THE CASES

Brazil

Brazil exemplifies why political affinity, along with prestige and national security, were important in influencing government political support for the nuclear industry. It also shows why prestige and national security formed a unique amalgamation of factors that was difficult, if not impossible, to disentangle. Because the prestige/national security factor itself had some effect on political affinity, we must discuss it first.

In an article on India's nuclear and space industries, Raju Thomas displays a chart that shows a continuum of countries, from those that had strong national security motivations for developing a nuclear industry to those countries for which such motivations were weak (Thomas 1986:3315–342). Thomas lists Brazil in the set of countries for which strategic concerns were relatively unimportant; he argues that if Brazil (or Argentina) sought to develop a nuclear industry, it was more for international prestige than for security reasons (Thomas 1986:315).

This view disregards not only the long-standing rivalry for power between Brazil and Argentina, but also how the Brazilian military – along with, as we will see, policymakers in other NICs – viewed "prestige." Myers contends that "internationally, Brazil aspired to recognition as the hegemonic power in South America as one of eight or so states with significant global interests" (Myers 1984:887). Yet, when Argentina signed an agreement with West Germany to transfer nuclear technology in 1968 – without many use restrictions or safeguards – Brazilian military leaders feared that Argentina might soon possess the technology needed to manufacture nuclear weapons. That, Myers notes, "in a single stroke could [have provided] Buenos Aires with the power and prestige necessary to challenge Brazil's influence in the buffer states of Uruguay, Paraguay, and Bolivia" (Myers 1984:890).

From the point of view of the Brazilian military leaders, if Brazil's prestige were challenged so successfully, its influence – and hence its national security – would be threatened. In this way, then, the two factors blended into one, and helped influence the Brazilian military government to support rapid acquisition of nuclear technology.

Further background and historical detail show how these prestige and national security concerns set the stage for the political affinity variable to influence outcomes. For ultimately, despite the military leaders' early enthusiasm, government political support for the nuclear industry declined greatly. Part of the explanation for this was that nuclear energy came to be seen as less vital as hydroelectric power emerged as an important alternative. But in this case, as with the others we will examine, the political affinity of the *corpo técnico* – composed essentially of scientists (most of whom were university professors) and *empresários* – was probably the most influential in determining the outcome.

In the Brazilian case, the political affinity between the scientists and the regime was particularly poor. As we will see, the evidence indicates that nuclear scientists[4] in Brazil had strong views in favor of democracy and were often highly critical of the military regime. And, unlike the Argentine case[5] (discussed below), Brazil's nuclear industry came to be strongly associated with the military and the overall military agenda. As a result, Brazil's nuclear scientists, with political characteristics similar to their counterparts in Argentina but operating under different circumstances, could not support the program. Without mutual political cooperation between scientists and government, and without a government tradition of giving the scientists more control of the program (which occurred in Argentina), Brazil's nuclear program had an unsuccessful political outcome.

Empresários as well as scientists (almost all of them university professors) objected not only to the nature of the program but also to the way in which the government went about developing it. Rather than consider the *corpo técnico*'s arguments in favor of a gradual development of indigenous technology, the government went ahead with an agreement with West Germany which, in the scientists' view, did not transfer sufficient essential technology. Moreover, to the dismay of the *empresários*, the agreement did not permit much participation by local firms. This last aspect of the agreement outraged many *empresários* who complained that they should at least have been included in the planning process. As for scientists, even when some individual members of the scientific community seemed to have convinced the government of the technological problems with the program, the scientists as a whole still refused to support it ("The Nuclear..." 1981:10; Adler 1987:326). Indeed, the very influential, 17,000–strong Brazilian Society for the Advancement of Science (SBPC), passed a motion which expressed suspicion of *any* program linked to the military ("The Nuclear..." 1981:10).

Thus, not only did the highly educated, democracy-oriented *corpo técnico* harbor antagonistic sentiments on principle about the military's being in power; it was also fed up with being excluded from the overall decisionmaking process. And this particular *corpo técnico* (unlike that in the pharmaceutical sector) was not likely passively to accept the *status quo*. As Girotti wrote, the opposition to the nuclear program among these groups became "part of the larger reaction against the character of the regime.... in other words, the Brazilian anti-nuclear opposition took place within the broader context of the fight for democracy" (Girotti 1984:196). In Brazil, as elsewhere in Latin America, those with special training and education – and the nuclear *corpo técnico* were easily among the elite of that category – sought to live up to the activist philosophy the SBPC advocated: "Today's scientist is a participating citizen, committed to improving the community around him" (Girotti 1984:198).

In order to understand more fully how international prestige, access, and – especially – political affinity affected government political support for the sector, we must examine some of the history behind the program. Such an examination will explain, as well, why scientists in the nuclear *corpo técnico* were excluded from decisionmaking, and why they became such strong opponents of the military regime's nuclear program.

The foundations for significant Brazilian involvement in development of nuclear technology began even before the advent of the military regime. Indeed, this involvement came about as early as the highly nationalist Kubitscheck Administration in the late 1950s, when the government established a special commission to establish directions for a Brazilian nuclear sector. Following the recommendations of the commission, in 1956 the Kubitscheck government set up the Atomic Energy Institute (IEA) at the University of São Paulo, as well as the National Commission on Atomic Energy (CNEN). The IEA's purpose was to promote research and the formation of human resources. CNEN was to serve as an administrative agency, setting policy for the sector.

In 1961, with Brazil still under civilian rule, the new President, Jânio Quadros, proposed that Brazil begin importing nuclear power stations in order to meet increased demands for electricity. Hence the 1963 government development plan called for construction of such plants, with as much participation on the part of Brazilian industry as possible (Rosa 1987:22–3). Thus, the military regime that took over after the 1964 coup was not itself responsible for the beginnings of the Brazilian nuclear industry; the industry had even earlier origins.

What the military governments that came to power after 1964 did do, however, was greatly expand and accelerate Brazil's involvement in the nuclear power industry, but *without* the active participation of key local *empresários* and scientists. It was during the military regime that the government's plan for purchasing a whole set of nuclear power plants took shape, and in this context that the German–Brazilian nuclear accord of 1975 was signed. Understanding these specific events is crucial to an explanation of the exclusion of the scientists.

In 1971 the CNEN created the Brazilian Nuclear Technology Company, which later became Brazilian Nuclear Companies, or Nuclebras. Nuclebras' function was to oversee the construction of the proposed power plants. The first, named Angra I for its location at Angra dos Reis in the state of Rio de Janeiro, was to be constructed by the US firm, Westinghouse. This project was to be a "turn-key" power plant; i.e., one that Westinghouse would design and build itself, requiring from the Brazilians only a "turn of the key" to have it begin operating. In fact, Brazilian participation in Angra I's construction was to be about 8 percent, but then only in such low-level activities as laying cement, or other non-technical aspects of construction (Adler 1987:311).

Brazilian scientists opposed this purchase of a turn-key nuclear power plant. No transfer of technology was included with the purchase. To make matters worse, the plant ran on enriched uranium, a substance that Brazil would have to import from the United States. This project, in the scientists' view, certainly did not seem the best way to develop nuclear technology in Brazil; it would make the country dependent on the US, which at that time was the sole exporter of nuclear technology and the enriched uranium fuel that was required to run the kind of reactor the government intended to purchase.

Mirow argues that military government officials went ahead with the project, despite the opposition of the scientists, because the alternative was to have a Candu kind of reactor, developed originally in Canada, which required only natural (not enriched) uranium. And to the military government, the Candu reactor – used in "underdeveloped" countries such as India and Argentina – had insufficient status (Mirow 1979:34). In this view, a Candu reactor would be inappropriate for a country such as Brazil, at that time at the height of its rapid-growth "economic miracle" period, which had the potential to become a world power. If this view is accurate, prestige had an especially strong influence on the military government's decisions at this point.

In 1974, however, the United States government – increasingly concerned about the diffusion of technology that could be used to manufacture nuclear weapons – prohibited Westinghouse from supplying Brazil with the nuclear technology for the manufacture of enriched uranium (Mirow 1979:36).[7] In 1972, when the Brazilian government had completed arrangements to buy the nuclear power plant from Westinghouse, importation of enriched uranium from the US had not been a problem. By 1974, however, Washington no longer permitted this (Mirow 1979:35). This situation posed a serious problem for Brazil, which now had a nuclear power plant but no way to make it operational. It was at about this time that Brazilian officials began to work out a deal with West Germany. By 1975 West German nuclear firms, notably Kraftwerk Union (KWU), convinced Brazilian diplomats and military leaders that the Germans should construct the next two power plants, Angra II and III, and six others for a total of eight by 1990. In exchange for the Brazilian government's purchase of the plants, the German firms would supply sufficient nuclear technology for Brazil eventually to be able to construct its own nuclear power plants, and to manufacture its own enriched uranium.

This agreement, known as the German–Brazilian accord, also dismayed the Brazilian nuclear scientists. Not having been consulted about the agreement or included in the negotiations with the Germans (this alone was upsetting), the scientists were not at all pleased with the agreement's terms. And opposition to the agreement on the part of the Brazilian scientists would grow even stronger over time.

The scientists' main complaint was that despite the claims that the accord would transfer highly advanced nuclear technology to Brazil, the possibility that any significant transfer of technology would take place was slim. In the nuclear scientists' view, Brazil was simply not equipped to absorb the technology Germany was offering. Brazil did not have enough nuclear specialists with advanced training (at the Master's and Ph.D. level) to take on this kind of rapid, massive transfer of highly sophisticated technological know-how and be able to assimilate it for indigenous projects. Moreover, a key element of the technology West Germany intended to transfer was as yet still experimental. This was the Becker "jet nozzle" technology, used in the enrichment of uranium. Finally, costs of the overall project – *eight* very expensive nuclear power stations (at a cost, according to a conservative estimate, of 10 billion, although some estimated the final cost would be closer to $40 billion) (Carvalho 1987:55) – weighed against the benefits (not that great when one realized that Brazil had abundant hydroelectric capability) seemed negligible.

The military regime disregarded the qualms of the scientists. Unfortunately, however, these concerns turned out to be valid. First, Brazil *was* unable effectively to absorb the nuclear technology. The lack of adequately trained personnel proved to be the most serious problem. Renowned Brazilian physicist and former CNEN president, Hervasio Guimarães de Carvalho, estimated that in order for the transfer to work, Brazil would need 10,000 individuals with the necessary technical training. But, by the early 1980s, Nuclebras' special training program had generated a total of only 2,459 engineers and technicians (Adler 1987:309–10). As Joaquim de Carvalho, former director for Nuclen (the technological branch of Nuclebras) remembered later:

> I was convinced that, in truth, there was no substantive transfer of technology in this area... [just] a transfer of experience in the area of coordination of nuclear power station assembly projects, which is also important, without doubt, but leaves us dependent in the more relevant areas of conception and basic engineering.
>
> (Carvalho 1987:52–3)

Another major concern of the scientists, the Becker "jet nozzle" technology, also proved to be very costly to operate and therefore inefficient. In fact, estimates were that merely operating the first uranium enrichment plant with this technology was going to *consume* 1.5 million kilowatt hours of electricity annually – as much as a medium-sized hydroelectric plant produced in one year (Myers 1984:892). By 1988, the Brazilian government had decided to dismantle all jet nozzle equipment in the country, and had set up new plants using the more standard ultra-centrifuge process. (By this time, the West German nuclear industry had already abandoned this technology) ("Uranium..." 1988:5).

Finally, the cost of the nuclear power plants soared as technical problems mounted. First, Angra I, not even part of the German–Brazilian agreement, had problems from the start. Not long before it was finally to begin functioning in 1982, vibrations in the generator forced it to be shut down. Even after it began functioning again, other problems kept it from operating at full capacity (Myers 1984:894). Similar technical problems plagued Angra II and III. Part of the reason for these difficulties related to the scientists' main concern, that Brazil was not adequately prepared to undertake the project; if it had been, it would have been able to avoid these problems. But the result was an enormous increase in the projected cost of completing the entire project. By 1985, all of Nuclebras' projects – despite the meager results – already constituted $2.1 billion of Brazil's $102 billion foreign debt (Adler 1987:317). Clearly, the country did not need a bigger debt, especially when, by the 1980s, Brazil's hydroelectric power potential appeared to be sufficient to meet the demand for electricity until the year 2020, at costs three times less than nuclear power (Carvalho 1987:51).

Given the enormity of the problems, it was not that surprising that the National Security Council, under the direct authority of President Figuereido (the last military president before the advent of civilian rule in 1985), finally acceded to some of the arguments of the nuclear scientists to scale back the program. Prominent nuclear physicist José Goldemberg, an opponent of the military's nuclear program whose political affinities lay with the opposition PMDB party, was instrumental in articulating the scientists' concerns ("The

Nuclear..." 1981:10). Franco Montoro, the opposition PMDB governor of the state of São Paulo, had already expressed firm opposition to two nuclear plants in his state, the proposed site of the next two to be built ("Brazil..." 1981:71). Montoro, however, whose political views were similar to José Goldemberg's[6], did more than merely give in reluctantly to Goldemberg's views; he put him in charge of all the important energy companies in the state of São Paulo ("Montoro..." 1983:4).[7]

In the end, the Brazilian government decided not to construct the remaining six reactors. It would stop with Angra III. And after 1985, the new civilian PMDB government in Brasilia, with its emphasis on social priorities, sought to move away from the large projects which had been such a central part of the military regime's agenda (*The Economist...*1985:12).

The future of the nuclear power program was very much in question, but certainly the military government's plans for the sector – facing strong opposition from those in the nuclear *corpo técnico* itself – seemed doomed. Indeed, much to the military's dismay, in 1990 President Collor revealed a secret military effort to develop nuclear weapons, and promised to put an end to it. There were rumors that the military's efforts would continue despite Collor's promise. But Collor made a point of putting his Minister of Science and Technology and that most prominent of nuclear *corpo técnico* members, José Goldemberg himself – as noted, a long-standing opponent of the military's nuclear program – in charge of Brazil's overall nuclear policy ("Collor's..." 1990). Finally, with the democratic transition, Brazil's nuclear *corpo técnico* was beginning to have some degree of influence.

Unlike the scientists and other technically trained individuals in the nuclear industry, those in the computer sector had not been excluded from decisionmaking, and did not have such a negative view of the military government's plans for the sector. Why were things so different in the nuclear industry? Having discussed the background to the nuclear industry, we can now analyze further the three variables we have mentioned throughout: international prestige, foreign ownership and technological dominance, and political affinity.

It is important to remember that the Brazilian military government had been frustrated in its attempts to acquire the complete nuclear fuel cycle[8] (including the ability to manufacture enriched uranium) from Westinghouse. Washington refused to permit such a transfer to a nation that would not sign the Nuclear Non-proliferation Treaty. Yet the Brazilian military believed that acquiring this capability was important if Brazil were to maintain its prestige and national security. Such concerns on the part of Brazil's military leaders were especially keen at the time of the signing of the German–Brazilian accord, for in 1974 India had exploded its own nuclear device. Meanwhile, Argentina already had one nuclear power station, and had begun construction on a second, both of which used natural uranium. Significantly, the spent fuel from natural uranium reactors could also be used to produce the ingredients needed to make nuclear bombs.

But because uranium enrichment technology was not of the sort that could be quickly developed locally – and for reasons of prestige Brazil's military leaders, as noted, refused to build natural uranium reactors – Brazil was forced to find another source. Brazilian leaders turned to West Germany, even though that meant relying on the experimental German technology, the only kind West Germany was willing to transfer. (West Germany had other kinds of technology for uranium enrichment, but was willing to sell only the unproven Becker "jet nozzle" process) (Myers 1984:892). Although in the nuclear industry the access variable did not, as noted, present an insurmountable obstacle to Brazil's development of indigenous technology, the military government's national security and prestige concerns kept it from following the slow gradual route undertaking such a task would entail. Hence the military accepted the West German offer of the unproven technology (with unfortunate results, as we will explain later).

It was for these reasons, then, that the scientists' concerns were neglected. It was for these reasons that the Brazilian National Security Council (CSN) kept such tight control over the military program. And it was for these reasons, as well, that the entire nuclear program took on the taint – in the nuclear scientists' view – of being closely linked with the military, and with the military's concerns. The CNEN, supposedly the administrative body for the Brazilian nuclear program, never became an instrument by which the scientists themselves could guide the course of the industry, independently from the military, as did Argentina's CNEA (to be discussed in a later section of this chapter). Even public discussion and debate over the direction the nuclear program should take, which would have permitted the scientists to make a strong case for their views, was expressly forbidden under the censorship the military regime imposed during much of the 1960s and 1970s.

All of this worked to reduce the political affinity of the nuclear *corpo técnico*[9] with those in the military regime. The actions and statements of key nuclear scientists associated with the program indicate the degree to which they distrusted and opposed the military regime's nuclear plans. For instance, Joaquim de Carvalho, a key figure as Director of Nuclebras' technological research subsidiary, Nuclen, quit and began a public campaign attacking the military government's nuclear program. Luiz Pinguelli Rosa, a physicist and at one time head of the Brazilian Society of Physicists (SBF), wrote numerous articles criticizing the Brazil–German nuclear agreement as flawed in its most basic premises. Criticizing the undemocratic way in which that decision had been made, he stressed that the issue of nuclear reactor safety should be decided in a more democratic fashion, with full public discussion and debate

(Rosa 1987:31–48).[10] Another physicist, Rogerio Cezar de Cerqueira Leite, perhaps the most renowned scientist in all of Brazil, also criticized the military's approach to developing the nuclear industry, expressing at the same time his strong distaste for the military regime itself. Noting that all the scientific and technical societies that had spoken out about the military's nuclear program had been "systematically" against it, he pointed out that scientists, businessmen, and others who opposed the military's nuclear plans during the military regime had, in doing so, "taken on the risks and accepted the consequences of confrontation with the [military] regime." (Leite 1987: 60–1) In Brazil in the mid-1970s, that sort of confrontation was in itself a kind of rebellious act against the military government.

José Goldemberg, of course, had taken the kind of risk Leite mentioned, and finally was able to persuade the Brazilian National Security Council, and the President of the Republic himself, General Figueireido, to alter the military's plans for the nuclear industry. By that time, however, the scientists' suspicions about the military regime had become so great that many of them did not accept the validity of the National Security Council's move (Adler 1987:326). Indeed, Goldemberg, President of the Brazilian Society for the Advancement of Science (SBPC) until 1980, probably had something to do with the SBPC's 1981 decision to pass a resolution expressing "concern at the support given by the government to nuclear projects with a clear military purpose," and its decision to inform the public of the true military agenda behind the government's nuclear program ("The Nuclear..." 1981:10). In the political context of the early 1980s in Brazil, such actions were risky in themselves.

In fact, these actions on the part of the SBPC are the most marked indication of the lack of political affinity between the scientists and the military regime. Clearly, the scientists, engineers, and *empresários* saw the military's nuclear program as serving a military purpose, in that it served the military's own interests more than those of the nuclear *corpo técnico*. In this way the government's program for the nuclear industry differed from that for the computer industry. While the military regime sought international prestige, the nuclear *corpo técnico* sought gradual, indigenous development for the Brazilian nuclear industry. And as the actions and statements of its members made evident time and again, the pro-democratic nuclear *corpo técnico* did not support the military government. Clearly, then, political affinity between those in power and the *corpo técnico* – the full cooperation and support of which was so important for the success of an endeavor as high-tech and complex as developing a local nuclear industry – was very low. In conjunction with the perceived military purpose behind the government's nuclear efforts, this lack of political affinity destroyed confidence in the Brazilian nuclear program, damaged its chances of success, and ultimately resulted in a low level of government political support for the nuclear industry in Brazil.[11]

Argentina

The Argentine nuclear industry case was similar to Brazil's in some ways. Prestige/national security concerns for the Argentine military leaders were analogous to those in Brazil. Political affinity between the nuclear *corpo técnico* and the government was very low as well. Unlike the Brazilian case, however, the Argentine *corpo técnico* obtained relatively high levels of government political support for indigenous technological development in the sector. The explanation for this outcome requires some historical background on the origins and development of the Argentine nuclear sector.

The National Atomic Energy Commission (CNEA) was key in creating a political haven for nuclear scientists that sheltered them from what would otherwise have been, for them, an unacceptable political environment in which to work. For this reason, it was central to the Argentine nuclear program's success. Created by the Argentine government in 1950, CNEA's purpose was to coordinate Argentina's indigenous research for the development of the nuclear energy industry. While under the broad control of the government since its inception, the agency was always non-partisan (Adler 1987; Poneman 1982). Ironically, in fact, its very "non-partisan" character was itself responsible for the agency's taking on a definite political orientation. Further elaboration here will help explain this apparent paradox.

Juan Peron, President of Argentina when the CNEA was created, was facing growing domestic political opposition in the early 1950s. Thus, when a former Nazi nuclear scientist, Ronald Richter, told him that he had developed a method of nuclear fission that could create virtually unlimited supplies of cheap, easily controlled energy, Peron jumped at the opportunity to make an announcement that might salvage his political fortunes. At the press conference at which he made the announcement, Peron proclaimed that he "wanted to inform the people of the Republic... of an event that will have a transcendent effect on their lives, and, no doubt, on the world" (Mariscotti 1985:26). Peron must have felt that making such a declaration would be sure to silence the opposition to his government.

Despite skepticism from scientists worldwide, Peron continued to use Richter's claims for political advantage. (As with the Brazilian military and its concerns about *international* prestige, this was a case in which *domestic* prestige concerns went awry.) Nevertheless, even Peron may have had some doubts about the veracity of Richter's claims, for the CNEA was established in 1950 partly to investigate the scientist's work (Poneman 1982:70). Finally, after several years (and US$70 million in research support) with no substantive results, Richter was fired and the program dismantled. That which Peron had intended to be a great political success had turned into a political fiasco. As a result of this incident, Peron refused to make the same mistake again. Thus, Poneman notes, he

> ordered the CNEA to hire qualified personnel, regardless of their political creed.... Largely due to the Richter affair, the Commission became a haven to anti-Peronists, providing a nonpartisan legacy which set the tone for much subsequent development of nuclear energy in Argentina.
>
> (Poneman 1982:70)

But Poneman and others[12] underemphasize that in fact the best nuclear scientists were "anti-Peronists," who looked with great disfavor upon Peron's undemocratic tendencies. The autonomy Peron had given the agency enabled the top nuclear scientists, *with their strong political orientation in favor of democracy*, to work enthusiastically for the nuclear program. Because the scientists could control CNEA's agenda, and keep its focus on nuclear energy rather than nuclear weaponry, they could continue to support it despite their dislike for the various authoritarian military governments under which it operated.

Emanuel Adler's data support this argument (although Adler himself takes a very different approach to it in seeking to support a different argument altogether). As Adler writes,

> Clearly, the success of Argentina's nuclear program was due to its civilian character, which fostered a sense of solidarity and purpose among the CNEA scientists.... Therefore, if Argentina did decide to make the bomb, it would kill the goose with the golden eggs – the ideological glue that holds the CNEA, one of its most successful institutions, together would dissolve.
>
> (Adler 1987:302)

Yet it was more than absence of partisan conflict among the scientists that accounted for the political success of the CNEA; it was their willingness to work in an environment which would not compromise their political views. If the CNEA had become an instrument of the military's agenda, these highly educated scientists, with their strong democratic values, simply would have been willing to support it no longer.

Beginning with Peron, then, the CNEA's autonomy from presidential political intervention became a tradition in Argentina, which continued with succeeding administrations. In this way the Argentine nuclear program did not suffer unduly from the turmoil and disruptions that beset Argentine society as a whole, and, in a kind of self-reinforcing, positive cycle of success, achieved objectives which encouraged subsequent governments to support the agency's work even more, which led to still further accomplishments and still more government political support.

For example, when Peron decided to have those working in the CNEA hired without regard to political orientation (which, in fact, meant anti-Peronist, pro-democracy scientists were employed), he appointed a Navy captain, Pedro Iraolagoitia, as CNEA president. Despite his links with the military,[13] Iraolagoitia carried out Peron's instructions well, and within three years had turned the Argentine nuclear power research program into a serious, viable endeavor (Poneman 1982:70). After Peron left office in 1955, this program continued, and the new CNEA President, Dr Oscar Quihillat, gave the CNEA even more autonomy in determining its own objectives.

With this relative autonomy from the military government's agenda, the CNEA was able to pursue a slow, gradual approach to the acquisition of nuclear technology. Far more concerned about avoiding dependence on imports of enriched fuel than was the Brazilian military regime, the CNEA made a point of building reactors that used natural uranium, rather than trying to move on to the so-called "advanced" enriched uranium reactors right away. The CNEA's more gradual approach was especially important in a field employing such sophisticated, complex technology, because it took so long for nuclear power plants to be built (especially when the CNEA was determined to use local industry as much as possible).

For instance, the CNEA study for Argentina's first nuclear power station (indeed, the first nuclear power station in all of Latin America), Atucha 1, was conducted in 1964. Although the plant had a projected finishing date of 1971, it was not actually finished and producing electricity until 1974. Part of the reason for the delay was the CNEA's insistence on using domestic technology and manufacturing capabilities wherever possible – a very different strategy from that pursued in Brazil, or, as we will discuss later, South Korea. For construction of the Atucha 1, for example, the CNEA had awarded the contract to the foreign supplier (the German firm Siemens) which allowed the highest degree of participation by local industry, nearly 40 percent. Westinghouse and General Electric submitted bids that would have cost the Argentine government less, but they were for enriched uranium technology (Tweedale 1982:87–8). The CNEA, of course, had already decided in favor of natural uranium technology.

One consequence of the continuity and autonomy within the CNEA, and, at least indirectly related to these factors, the accomplishments of the nuclear program, was that there was not a great deal of political controversy over the presence of a nuclear program in Argentina, either among decisionmakers or within the general population. In the case of Atucha 1, the project was so obscure that top decisionmakers made decisions about choice of reactor types, selection of foreign suppliers, etc., behind closed doors but – an important point – with strong guidance from the CNEA scientists. For decisions on construction of the second reactor, the public was more involved in debate, but it was a debate limited to these same kinds of issues, and not about whether Argentina should have a nuclear program or not. The scientists, able to guide the program in the directions they thought best, had no reason to speak out against it and seek public support to have it overturned.

But the political autonomy that had been the prerequisite for the nuclear program's achievements disappeared with Peron's return from exile in 1973. This time Peron reversed his earlier stance, and filled the CNEA with his own political allies, in the process replacing about 60 of the agency's top officials. The result was to bring decisionmaking in the CNEA, and the entire nuclear program itself, to a virtual standstill (Poneman 1982:76–7). Many top scientists left the program in disgust. Such problems continued during the presidency of Peron's wife, Isabel, who succeeded him upon his death in 1974, and great numbers of the CNEA scientists and officials left the agency. By the end of Isabel's Administration, the CNEA had no autonomy from presidential or outside political intervention whatsoever; every policy decision of any kind required an executive decree.

Ironically, only with the military coup of 1976 was autonomy restored to the CNEA and the nuclear program revived. Another Navy captain, this one a *bona fide corpo técnico* member with a Ph.D. in nuclear physics, was installed in the CNEA presidency. Many of the Peronist political appointees were fired, and many who had been in the CNEA before returned. The supposedly apolitical (although in fact pro-democratic) character of the agency, and the government's non-interventionist relations with it, were restored.

With the "hands off" relationship established once again, the CNEA could swing back into action to maintain the viability of indigenous research efforts. As a result, government commitment to nuclear power continued strong and steady (as evidenced by presidential decrees in 1977 calling for the attainment of complete self-sufficiency in the nuclear power industry). And in 1978, the CNEA presented a 15–year plan for the industry, which a government-appointed inter-ministerial commission approved. It provided for the CNEA to construct four new nuclear reactors, as well as to build any equipment necessary for Argentina to have the indigenous technological capability to run the complete nuclear fuel cycle (including manufacture of enriched uranium and reprocessing of spent fuels) by 1997 (Poneman 1982:79).

As Poneman points out, "[t]hat such a major plan was approved despite Argentina's relentless economic plight documents the depth of the political commitment to nuclear power" (Poneman 1982:79). Clearly, this plan was a testament to the government's strong political support for the CNEA's efforts to attain self-sufficiency in the nuclear industry.

South Korea

The South Korean government pursued a strategy very different from that of the Argentine government. In an approach more similar to that of the Brazilian military, the (former) South Korean military government entered the nuclear industry by having foreign firms manufacture turn-key plants. Thus, government political support for the development of indigenous nuclear technology was initially very low. Also in contrast to the Argentine case, the South Korean military government maintained tight control and guidance over the direction of the nuclear program.

Despite these facts, the South Korean government's approach to the nuclear industry did not provoke much protest from the nuclear *corpo técnico*. The South Korean case is an anomaly in that political affinity was not, directly or indirectly, for better or worse, a significant factor in determining government political support for the South Korean nuclear industry.

In order to understand why this was so, and to what extent prestige/national security, access, and political affinity played a role, we need to examine the development of the South Korean nuclear industry in greater detail. In doing so, we will also consider whether the South Korean government's approach was merely short sighted or, in fact, represented an alternative model for industrial development.

The South Korean government developed its nuclear program very rapidly. As early as 1958, the government had worked out a deal to buy a small research reactor from the General Dynamics corporation, and by 1959 had set up its own Office of Atomic Energy (OAE), under the direct supervision of the president, to administer the program. Under the administrative embrace of the OAE were the Atomic Energy Commission (AEC), which guided OAE policy, and the Atomic Energy Research Institute (AERI), which conducted atomic research. These agencies were dominated by scientists who proposed plans for the sector and recommended that South Korea should, indeed, pursue a nuclear program as the country had few resources of hydroelectric power, coal, or oil (Ha 1983:82–109).

While the scientists had a role at this beginning stage of the program in discussing technical matters, the kinds of training programs that would be needed, etc., the military government dominated the decisionmaking process. In 1962 the government established a committee to develop a nuclear power plan. This committee, composed of representatives of such government-linked agencies as the OAE, the state-run Korea Electric Company (KECO), and the Ministry of Commerce and Industry, urged the government to construct nuclear power plants to meet South Korea's future energy needs. Later, in 1965, another committee, the Council on Nuclear Power Generation, composed essentially of representatives from the same government-linked agencies (including the universities, also controlled by the government), urged the government to construct two nuclear power plants in the 1970s. Finally, in 1968, the government established a council with decisionmaking capacity, the Council for the Promotion of Nuclear Power Generation. Significantly, *this* Council, composed of government technocrats, actually made the decision to construct two nuclear reactors, and assigned different government agencies the tasks of carrying the project out. Unlike the Argentine government, however, the South Korean leaders did not intend to put the emphasis on indigenous research and development for the construction of these plants – at least, not in the beginning. Like Brazil, South Korea put out bids for foreign firms to build the plants, with little concern for domestic content.

Westinghouse received the first contract to build a turn-key plant, as well as most of the contracts that followed. By 1979 – as Brazil was experiencing a panoply of difficulties in getting its first three nuclear power plants even partially completed – South Korea had four nuclear power plants under construction. And the program continued to move rapidly, with 12 plants built or under construction by 1987 ("Seoul's..." 1987:46–7). The first three of these, however, were almost entirely foreign-built plants, made largely with foreign technology.

After the construction of the first three plants, the government made the decision to increase the domestic technological contribution of those to follow. In addition to imposing domestic content quotas on subsequent plants, the government planned to begin investing in earnest in the development of indigenous nuclear technology (over $100 million from 1977 to 1981) and established an agency called Korean Nuclear Services, Inc. (KNE) to promote research in this area (Ha 1983:96–7). At the same time, the AERI continued its program (begun in 1968) to train designers, engineers, and technicians to operate the nuclear power plants, and take part in the development and construction of these plants (Ha 1983:90).

Given the response of the Brazilian nuclear *corpo técnico* to the Brazilian military government's nuclear program, it seems surprising, at first, that the South Korean nuclear *corpo técnico* had not expressed similarly strong opposition to what – up until this point – had been a disregard for indigenous technological development in the nuclear industry. Yet, in South Korea there were no resignations of prominent scientists; there were no public campaigns waged against the government's plan. And indeed, no significant protest of this kind arose throughout the development of the military government's nuclear program. Why was the political affinity variable, so much a factor (when it could not be controlled) in the other cases, not present here?

The answer has to do, in part, with the relatively small size of the nuclear *corpo técnico* in South Korea. In 1958, before the government's nuclear plan began, there were only 78 scientists working in the nuclear field (Ha 1983:83). Although many more had received training since then, especially after the AERI's training program had gone into effect, the number of technically trained personnel was still very small.[14] Moreover, the South Korean nuclear *corpo técnico* members were less established than their counterparts in Brazil. Certainly South Korea did not have nearly the number of renowned, highly respected nuclear physicists that Brazil had. Nor did South Korean physicists and engineers have powerful, highly respected, and well-organized scientific and technical societies like the Brazilian SBF and SBPC to serve as a kind of lobbying group for their cause.

But, most important in determining the relative lack of political opposition from *corpo técnico* members, or other would-be opponents of the South Korean government's nuclear plans, was the particularly authoritarian nature of the South Korean political system. At least until the late 1980s, there was little or no public debate about these issues, and the population as a whole had virtually no information about the kinds of decisions that were being made. Thus there was not really a broader society to whom the *corpo técnico* could appeal (in the way the Brazilian computer and nuclear *corpos técnicos* did) for political opposition to the programs.[15]

Having made these observations, we should emphasize that our discussion thus far has presumed certain things about the South Korean nuclear *corpo técnico*. We have assumed that the Korean nuclear scientists and industrialists were *not* in favor of the military government's approach to the nuclear industry. Given the evidence from the other cases of the strong support for gradual, indigenous technological development among nuclear scientists in Brazil and Argentina, this seems to be a reasonable assumption. Furthermore, given the lost business opportunities domestic South Korean business faced as a result of the government's openness to foreign technology, it also seems reasonable to assume that the industrialists would not be in favor of the military government's nuclear plans.

More important than all of this, however, was that – unlike the Brazilian military – the South Korean military government was *not* following the approach that it did primarily as a quick way to get into the nuclear power industry. Rather, this approach represented an alternative development model. The military government permitted turn-key projects for a time. But after a certain period had passed, it sought to move beyond this. Amsden, in an analysis of the South Korean development model, describes South Korea's approach to industrial development, like those of other late industrializers such as Japan and Taiwan, as "a process of industrialization whose central tendency is *learning* rather than invention or innovation" (Amsden 1989:4). From learning about the turn-key projects, from operating them, from participating in international conferences about them, South Korea eventually, rather than creating the requisite technology on its own, could *learn* how to construct nuclear power plants, adapting the foreign technology to its own needs. Hence, contrary to the tendency in Latin American NICs to use protectionism to foster indigenous technology, initial encouragement of foreign turn-key projects could lead to future expansion of local technological capabilities. This was very much like what happened with the South Korean nuclear case.

This sort of model worked well for authoritarian, state-centric South Korea. It was doubtful, however, that it could work for Brazil, even Brazil under authoritarian rule. South Korea had the luxury, in a sense, to have a "learning period" because of the state's high degree of autonomy from social groups, including the nuclear *corpo técnico*. The scientists, a small, poorly-established group, could not oppose the South Korean state even if they wanted to. Not even the much more powerful industrialists could challenge the state's autonomy successfully. If the state perceived the long-term interests of South Korean economic development as being served best by an initially very receptive approach to foreign technology in the nuclear sector, then it had the capability to carry out its plans in this sector with a minimum of domestic opposition.

Brazil was different in that scientists and industrialists were becoming more powerful as democratization continued. Yet, even under authoritarian rule, Brazilian state autonomy had never been as great as that of South Korea. Beginning in 1987, South Korea, too, was undergoing the process of democratization. Nevertheless, the nature of the South Korean domestic structure meant that state autonomy would remain far greater in South Korea than in Brazil for some time to come. Thus, South Korea's alternative development model should continue to be effective.

CONCLUSIONS

Having analyzed some of the key cases, we can now present the results in Table 6.1.

As the table reveals at a glance, the political affinity variable was relevant in all of the cases examined here (with the exception of South Korea). Furthermore, the detailed discussion in the cases reveals that the political affinity variable, where present, played a very important role.

In Argentina and South Korea, government political support for indigenous technological development did not decline during the democratic transition period. In Argentina, a kind of artificially created political insulation of the *corpo técnico* worked to prevent the political affinity variable from becoming an obstacle. In South Korea, the relative strength of the state

Table 6.1   Relevant independent variables across cases

	Country		
	Brazil	*Argentina*	*South Korea*
Computers	1,2	No data	No data
Pharmaceuticals	1,2	No data	No data
Nuclear	1,2,3	1,2,3	1

Key:
1 = access variable
2 = political affinity variable
3 = prestige/national security variable

vis-à-vis society meant that the influence of the political affinity variable was virtually nil. In Brazil, however, there were none of these compensating factors to override the definite lack of political affinity between a military government pursuing a nuclear program with strongly authoritarian and military overtones, and the decidedly pro-democratic nuclear scientists. In the Brazilian case, therefore, the influence of political affinity was forceful and – in terms of the consequences for the government's nuclear program – disastrous.

As noted, the South Korean case was something of an anomaly. Also, the South Korean nuclear industry received higher levels of government political support, and had far more favorable economic outcomes than the nuclear industry in the other countries. We will examine the implications of the South Korean case further, in the context of a broader discussion of alternative models of industrial development, in the next chapter.

Another observation that is important to make here, is that comparison of political outcomes for the cases in this chapter with those for the primary cases, discussed in Chapters 2 and 3, demonstrates that the political affinity variable operated in different ways in different contexts. In the Brazilian computer and pharmaceutical cases, the relative degree of political affinity affected the respective *corpos técnicos'* abilities to gain the political support of the PMDB politicians. In the nuclear cases examined here, however, political affinity was important not only in this way but also – very much so – in influencing the extent of the willing and enthusiastic support of the *corpo técnico* members for industrial development programs.

The results of the Brazilian and Argentine nuclear cases perhaps best illustrate the importance of this aspect of the political affinity variable. In Brazil, without strong *corpo técnico* support for various government projects in the industry, prospects for favorable outcomes were dismal. In Argentina, where political affinity between the *corpo técnico* and the dominant political coalition was no more favorable than in Brazil, the political insulation of the *corpo técnico* from the successive military regimes kept this factor from becoming a significant problem.

7 Conclusion

This book has tried to establish that political affinity was important in the two primary cases examined here, as well as in the additional cases drawn from other industries and countries. It was relevant, but in different ways, during both the authoritarian period and the democratic transition. This difference in the way the variable operated during these two periods calls us to comment on the differences in policymaking under authoritarian regimes and during times of democratic transition, and on the future prospects for policymaking in the NICs. We will also consider a range of alternative models (with respect to the political affinity factor) for industrial policy in the NICs, and the extent to which NICs such as Brazil can make use of alternative approaches to overcome negative consequences of the political affinity factor.

During the authoritarian regime in Brazil, policy tended to be directed from the top down. The adjectives that applied to the Brazilian political system applied, of course, to the manner in which policy was made as well: hierarchical, corporatist, bureaucratic-authoritarian, patrimonial, organic-statist, clientelistic. Despite the dominating influence of the highest levels of the state apparatus *vis-à-vis empresários*, mid-level *técnicos*, and university professors during this period, however, the political affinity variable still had an influence on outcomes.

As Chapter 3 demonstrated, the political characteristics of the pharmaceutical *corpo técnico* members made them, on the whole, as passive and quiescent during the military years as they were during the later democratic transition period. The Profarma case revealed the extent to which the pharmaceutical *corpo técnico* allowed the government to set the policy agenda during this period, even when this meant that policies to promote industrial development in the pharmaceutical sector would ultimately be weakened and rendered ineffective in the face of international pressures.

The impact of political affinity on the nuclear industry during the military years was somewhat different. In this case, the lack of political affinity between the military regime and nuclear *corpo técnico* members during the military period inhibited *corpo técnico* members' willing and enthusiastic participation in important projects in the sector. This reluctance on the part of the nuclear *corpo técnico* to go along with the government's development plans for this sector obstructed the political success of the endeavour.

While the computer *corpo técnico*, having a similarly low degree of political affinity with the military regime, would seem to have faced the same difficulties as its counterpart in the nuclear industry during the military years, certain factors prevented this problem from occurring. Highly significant was the fact that the military officials working with the computer *corpo técnico* members were themselves somewhat different from the Brazilian military as a whole. Despite their military credentials, such officials as Frigate Captain José Guaranys (the official assigned to the original government project to develop a Brazilian computer), Colonel José Ezil Veiga da Rocha (Executive Director of SEI, 1985–7), and Colonel Edson Dytz (Executive Director of SEI, 1984–5), had political characteristics that were not that much different from the *corpo técnico* members themselves; indeed, these individuals would have to be classified as part of the *corpo técnico*.

In the nuclear industry, in contrast, there was a great divergence between the *corpo técnico* members and the high-ranking military ministers and other military officials responsible for the program. In this sector, the government's prestige/national security concerns predominated over all others. Hence, those responsible for making and approving policy for the nuclear sector did not themselves share many characteristics, in terms of education or political views, with the *corpo técnico* members. The problems inherent in this kind of distant relationship were exacerbated because, unlike the computer *corpo técnico*, the nuclear *corpo técnico* had little control over government policy in this area. Lacking political affinity with the military leaders to begin with, and prevented (because of the predominance of the military regime's prestige/national security concerns) from exerting significant control over policy, the nuclear *corpo técnico* was very suspicious of the government's nuclear program. Without the strong participation of this vital element, success of the program was greatly inhibited.

By the time Brazil had shifted to civilian government, the nuclear projects had significantly declined; hence our analysis of outcomes for this sector does not extend beyond the end of the military years. (Political activities on the part of the nuclear *corpo técnico* occurred as the democratization process was beginning to get underway in earnest, in the late 1970s and early 1980s.) However, as shown in Chapter 3, the lack of political affinity between the pharmaceutical *corpo técnico* and the new civilian politicians became especially significant during the democratic transition period. The pharmaceutical *corpo técnico* – unlike its counterpart in the computer industry – lacked the political affinity to make use of new opportunities presented by this shift in the nature of the regime. The computer *corpo técnico*, in contrast – as we saw in Chapter 2 – was able to make use of the democratic transition period to maintain and even increase government political support for the sector. Because the computer case reveals some important aspects of the differences in policymaking in high-technology industries during authoritarian and democratic regimes, it merits further discussion in this context.

The literature on democratization in Latin America emphasizes the enduring elements of the top-down, hierarchical, patrimonial, clientelistic, and essentially *non-democratic* tradition within Latin American nations after transitions to civilian rule (O'Donnell, Schmitter, Whitehead 1986; Stepan 1988; Baloyra 1987; Selcher 1986; Levine 1988:376–94; Mainwaring, O'Donnell, Valenzuela 1992). While there is some validity to this view, much of the theoretical literature that exists on the subject at this time was written *before* many of the transitions to civilian rule had taken place, and virtually none of it considers high-technology industrial policy separately from policymaking as a whole. Recent evidence on government policy toward the computer industry during (and after) the democratic transition, as presented in this book, strongly indicates that some prevalent ideas on democratization in Latin America, as well as on the prospects for favorable outcomes for the Latin American NICs in high technology sectors, need to be modified.

With the coming of the democratic transition, the computer *corpo técnico* managed to persuade the rising PMDB politicians to continue to support programs such as the market reserve and special subsidies for the computer sector. Thus, in this sector, at least, policy initiatives were *not* coming from the top down, in hierarchical fashion, as orders from the executive branch without input of any kind from "society" – i.e., businessmen, university professors, etc. working in the sector. To the contrary, "society," as represented by the computer *corpo técnico*, was in this instance lobbying the government to support a particular policy. That this effort was successful was of special note, because, as discussed in Chapter 2, the civilian politicians had initially been hostile to any such programs, seeing them as linked too closely to the military regime.

These events certainly did not mean that Brazil had become, or was even on the way to becoming, a pluralist democracy on the order of those in Western Europe or the United States. In most other areas, even in other high-technology sectors, such as pharmaceuticals, policy was not being made in this way. And certainly, the political successes of that small and rather elite segment of Brazilian society – the computer *corpo técnico* – did not guarantee that the poor majority of the Brazilian population would now be able to participate to the fullest extent in Brazilian government. What it did mean, however, as this book has argued and attempted to demonstrate throughout, was that because of the political affinity between the *corpos técnicos* of certain high technology sectors and politicians in NIC regimes were undergoing democratic transitions, industrial policy in these countries could diverge from what most scholars expected to be the enduring authoritarian pattern.

In any case, it is important to note that the kind of unexpected outcomes that occurred with respect to the Brazilian computer industry were most likely to happen during and shortly after the transition to democracy, and would not necessarily continue indefinitely after the democratic regime had been installed. During transition periods, those politicians coming into power were most frequently the very same who had been instrumental in opposing the former military regime in the first place. This fact meant that they tended to have particular political characteristics that gave them a high degree of political affinity with the computer *corpo técnico*: strong beliefs in democratic rule, desire to change the *status quo*, a civilian, democratic orientation more focused on social concerns. After the period of transition to democratic rule, however, the new democratic regime had at least the potential to take on a different political cast. Just because politicians were now democratically elected, and were part of a civilian rather than military regime, this did not necessarily mean that they would have a high degree of political affinity with the *corpo técnico* which had been so influential earlier.

The Brazilian case itself, of course, demonstrated this. PMDB politicians were the rising force in the National Congress during the peak of the transition period (latter years of the military regime), and the dominant force after the 1986 congressional elections. But in March, 1990, Fernando Collor, a strict economic conservative whose political views were anathema to many key computer *corpo técnico* members, became President of Brazil. In his wake he brought a wave of supporters to the National Congress with the new *deputados* elected later that year. Moreover, by this time (after the *Cruzado* Plan fiasco and the escalating rates of inflation), the PMDB had become almost completely discredited. Thus the computer *corpo técnico* no longer had a high degree of political affinity with the political characteristics of the dominant political coalition within the Brazilian government, and its political clout was consequently reduced.

The problems that can be associated with political affinity (or lack thereof) lead us to discuss ways Brazil and other NICs might be able to avoid such problems. We will conclude with some thoughts on the broader implications of our analysis for development and democratization in the NICs.

ALTERNATIVE MODELS (WITH RESPECT TO THE POLITICAL AFFINITY FACTOR) FOR INDUSTRIAL POLICY

In Chapter 6 we examined the influence of political affinity in South Korea and Argentina, countries with models of industrial development different in many respects from that of Brazil. Here we will consider these cases with regard to the influence political affinity might have in several different models of industrial policy.

Luiz Carlos Bresser Pereira, an economist and former Minister of Finance in Brazil, argues that there are at least three approaches to government intervention in Latin America (and, we might add, in the NICs generally) (Pereira forthcoming). One approach is populism, the doling out of government handouts and patronage for the political benefit of those in control of the budgetary apparatus. This mode of government intervention, used all too frequently in Latin America until recently, has been a cause of many of the economic difficulties the region has been struggling to overcome; clearly, it should be avoided.

Another approach, about which Bresser Pereira also has qualms, is what he calls "the Washington Consensus" approach. This approach is that espoused in the neoliberal policy prescriptions of the International Monetary Fund and many policymakers in Washington. It calls for drastically reduced government intervention in the economy, even if such reductions result in cuts for government funding for R&D or for policies to promote industrial development in strategic sectors.

The mode of government intervention to which Bresser Pereira himself adheres is what he calls the "Social Democratic" approach. This approach, too, calls for reducing the size of the state, but only to make it more efficient. Government intervention for the development of human and physical resources and even for limited protectionism, with a clearly defined strategic rationale, is seen as viable and essential in order to promote long-term economic development.

If the NICs are to overcome the obstacles posed by their position in the world economy, then clearly some form of government intervention, akin to Bresser Pereira's "Social Democratic" approach, is needed. What our discussion of the political affinity factor has shown, however, is that effective implementation of industrial policies to promote development can be helped or hindered by the degree of political affinity between industrial *corpos técnicos* and the dominant political elite. The question we need to address here, then, is what model for industrial development best takes this factor into account.

With this question in mind, we will consider some of the ways in which different models for industrial policy – as represented by our very different cases of South Korea, Brazil, and Argentina – have dealt with this issue.

South Korea

If we consider a range of models of industrial policy in terms of the impact the political affinity variable might have, one might be a model in which political affinity would have minimal influence. The South Korean model, because of its highly centralized, authoritarian nature, is a close approximation of this approach.

The most striking characteristics of the South Korean model of industrial policy are the aspects that made the political affinity variable virtually irrelevant: the very strong autonomy and unity of the state. With respect to autonomy, Evans notes that the years of Japanese colonial rule before World War II prevented the emergence of a strong "industrial bourgeoisie" to challenge the state after the Japanese withdrew from the country (Evans 1987:203–26). Gordon White and Robert Wade point out that the state prevented other kinds of autonomous social groups from emerging as well. For this reason, the South Korean state does not have to contend today with organized labor, industrial associations, or elected legislatures to the extent that governments in Latin American countries do (White,Wade 1988:10). Under these circumstances, the issue of political affinity was insignificant.

The South Korean state is unified in the sense that power is highly centralized. Control over most economic policy decisions is centered in one government agency, the Economic Planning Board (EPB). As a result, bureaucratic squabbles between departments of the government are rare. Contributing to the South Korean state's unity has been the real military threat posed by South Korea's hostile neighbor, North Korea. A strong incentive for economic development as a means of national defense, this threat has given centralized state power greater legitimacy (Bunge 1982:111).

The unity and autonomy of the South Korean state have enabled it to use a variety of policy mechanisms to promote economic growth. Although South Korea has primarily a market economy – approximately 70 percent of total investments are from private firms (Kwack 1986:69) – the relationship between government and business is very close. This relationship is marked, as a World Bank economist noted, by "selective government interventions across a wide range of activities, interventions that go beyond the creation of market (non-discretionary) incentives" (Westphal 1982:36). In order to co-ordinate the public and private sectors into a cohesive development program, South Korean leaders formulate comprehensive, five-year national economic plans. Among the means the government uses to implement these plans are the state's control over the budget; governmental domination of the banking system; the selective importation of technology; and other, less formal kinds of intervention (e.g., presidential telephone calls to the heads of major firms). Clearly, in a country such as South Korea, the strength of the state *vis-à-vis* society meant that the access and political affinity variables could not really play a role. Although the liberalization and elections of recent years indicate a shift toward more democratic rule, the merging of two important opposition parties with the ruling Democratic Justice Party in February, 1990, demonstrates the extent to which central authority still prevails. Not having to deal with the kinds of political obstacles the access and political affinity variables presented in other NICs has served South Korea well; for as Chalmers Johnson notes, "[p]olitical leaders attempting to implement a long-term industrial policy must... have the capacity to depoliticize in part their key economic decisions" (Johnson 1987:152). South Korea's Economic Planning Board, and the rest of South Korea's unified and autonomous state bureaucracy, provided this capacity.

Brazil

The Brazilian state, like its Latin American counterparts, did not have these same capabilities. Certainly it was not as unified or autonomous as the South Korean state. While the South Korean government was able to define and accomplish long-range, comprehensive policy objectives very effectively, in Brazil merely proposing such objectives would likely have provoked intense political and bureaucratic struggles. The nature of the Brazilian state was characterized well in the title of highly respected Brazilian political scientist Sergio Abranches's dissertation on the subject, "The Divided Leviathan" (Abranches 1976). Such a state lends itself – for good or for ill – to the influence of such factors as access and political affinity.

The kinds of bureaucratic struggles that hindered the efforts to establish a viable program for the national pharmaceutical industry illustrate the Brazilian state's lack of unity. The *técnicos* in CEME developed proposals to promote the development of indigenous technology and a genuinely Brazilian pharmaceutical industry. Unlike EPB technocrats in South Korea, however, CEME had no control over foreign investments in the sector. Other *técnicos* in the Industrial Development Council (CDI), with whom prominent CEME *técnicos* disagreed about such matters, were in charge of this.

While these differences alone tended to inhibit the formulation of cohesive, long-range plans for the sector, bureaucratic disputes at the ministerial level were even more severe. While the Ministry of Industry and Commerce, Ministry of Health, and the Ministry of Social Welfare supported CEME's proposals, the Ministry of Finance and the Ministry of Planning – which were attempting to renegotiate Brazil's foreign debt – sought to do anything they could to avoid antagonizing foreign creditor governments. This, of course, included fighting against a proposal that had caused several of these same governments to threaten to make the debt negotiations difficult if the proposal were not withdrawn. In the end, as Chapter 3 showed, the bureaucratic needs of the Planning and Finance ministries prevailed over those of the other ministries.

The dispute between the government agency in charge of the computer market reserve policy, the *Secretaria de Informática* (SEI), and the agency in charge of the Free Zone of Manaus (Surframa), as discussed in Chapter 5, is another clear example of "the divided Leviathan." Aware of the way the free trade zone in Manaus, with all of its incentives for foreign investment and manufacture of foreign goods, had virtually eliminated indigenous industry in consumer electronics, SEI had to fight against permitting foreign computer firms to gain a substantial competitive edge in the Brazilian market by means of Manaus. The computer *corpo técnico* was able to use its political affinity with key PMDB politicians in order to prevent the government from providing highly attractive financial incentives to foreign computer firms for moving to Manaus. However, the computer *corpo técnico* could not prevent the foreign firms from obtaining access to the Brazilian market in some fields to which they had previously been denied access altogether.

Another bureaucratic struggle involving the computer sector, as discussed in Chapter 5, was the dispute between SEI and the Ministry of Communications (Minicom). Almost from the beginning, Minicom wanted to dismantle the market reserve in order to import the best, cheapest, and most state-of-the-art computer/telecommunications equipment available on the international market. Given the relatively high price of Brazilian computer products, Minicom gained many supporters to its cause over time.

The Brazilian state lacked autonomy as well as unity. But during the military regime, at least, the nature of state–society relations in Brazil, known as state corporatism, helped the state maintain some degree of autonomy. State corporatism encompassed a number of government intitiatives begun during the Vargas Administration in the 1930s and strengthened and modified during the military regime from 1964–85. Specifically, in order to reduce pressures from labor, industry, and other powerful social groups, the state had organized these groups into separate, hierarchical, officially sanctioned organizations. Organized into officially recognized labor organizations, workers, for example, would be more inclined to follow their official representatives. In this way, their demands could be more easily regulated and kept within predictable and reasonable limits.

While state corporatism gave the Brazilian state more autonomy than it otherwise would have had, it still had nowhere near the autonomy of the South Korean state. The Brazilian state never had control of the Brazilian banking system; it could not restructure entire industries by ordering them to coalesce into one firm for the sake of the country, etc. Thus, given the Brazilian state's relative lack of unity and – despite state corporatism – relative lack of autonomy, adoption of the South Korean model seemed out of the question. When low degrees of access (as in pharmaceuticals) and lack of political affinity (as in the nuclear sector) inhibited the government's political support for high-technology industries, the unity and autonomy of the state was insufficient to overcome these obstacles.

Argentina

Another, less structurally radical alternative (that is, one that would not require overcoming the obstacles presented by the structure of the Brazilian state apparatus and political culture) was needed. One alternative was that approach suggested by the Argentine experience with the nuclear industry, as discussed in Chapter 6. This kind of alternative is only useful, however, in cases in which the government already wishes to support the development of a particular sector, but – because of low degrees of political affinity between the *corpo técnico* and the dominant political coalition – cannot obtain the cooperation of the *corpo técnico*.

An organizational structure or framework can be set up whereby the program on which the *corpo técnico* is working is insulated from the political oversight and whims of the dominant political coalition. In the Argentine case, this sort of independence from the dominant regime was sufficient to enable the *corpo técnico* to participate fully and enthusiastically in the program. While the applicability of this kind of model is limited,[1] it could provide a solution in instances in which the necessary conditions (as described) apply, and a lack of political affinity is proving to be a major obstacle.

CONCLUSIONS

Concerns about political affinity in high-technology industries undergoing democratization may have even broader significance than the effectiveness of a particular country's development model. Indeed, as mastery of advanced, complex technological processes become progressively more essential to any nation's survival in the modern world economy, political affinity between *corpos técnicos* and governments will come to play an even more central role.

In a recent article, Robert Bates argues that, at the later stages of a society's economic development, highly educated human beings with advanced training become the key form of economic capital. Because such individuals are so crucial to a nation's ability to achieve economic growth, they have a great deal of bargaining power *vis-à-vis* the government. In this context, therefore, "those who possess skills and talents must be listened to, their needs made known, and their environment then structured so that they will happily do what they do best" (Bates 1991:26–7). The way to do this, Bates argues, is to let these people themselves make the key decisions about what they are doing – i.e., to let them have the authority to make decisions about the particular project or program with which they are involved. Bates suggests that this sort of process, carried out on a wide scale, was an important factor in bringing about peaceful transitions to democracy in Eastern Europe. Governments seeking economic growth gave up power "to those who control the key resource: the people themselves" (Bates 1991:27).

Something like this, but on a more limited scale, did seem to be occurring in some of the cases we have examined here. In Argentina, Peron came to realize that the nuclear scientists themselves would need to have a great deal of control over Argentina's nuclear program if he were to obtain the whole-hearted cooperation of the very best scientists, most of whom opposed his military regime. In Brazil, in contrast, the military government refused to cede control over the nuclear program to the scientists, and indeed refused even to listen to their advice. As a result of these varying approaches, the outcome for the Argentine nuclear industry was much more favorable than that for the Brazilian nuclear sector. The outcome of Brazil's nuclear program – especially when measured against the military's enormously optimistic original expectations – was very poor indeed, and hastened the military's return to the barracks. Such concerns are even more important for the NICs. In such countries, those with advanced technical training – as members of the relatively small, highly educated elite – are even more important, and tend generally to have far more political clout, than they do in the industrialized nations. (Of course, this assertion applies only in situations in which there is already a high degree of access and political affinity.)

Thus, NIC governments seeking to improve their position in the world economy – and in particular, those undergoing the process of democratization – must pay heed to the issues analyzed here. New opportunities for access during periods of democratization can give the political affinity variable special influence. Under favorable circumstances, political affinity can have a positive impact on government political support for a given industry; under other conditions, it can have a highly negative effect. Certainly, however, it should never be ignored.

Appendix I
The survey

The survey results in Chapter 4 are based on a sample of 80 individuals in the computer and pharmaceutical *corpos técnicos*. While this sample was not random, I did take care to ensure that those who received the survey were representative of the two *corpos técnicos* as a whole. For instance, of the total of 190 questionnaires I sent out, roughly equal proportions went to *empresários*, *técnicos*, and university professors in both sectors.

I chose recipients primarily from members of the main lobbying groups in each of the sectors. In the computer industry this was Abicomp; in the pharmaceutical sector, I sent the questionnaire – in numbers proportionate to the numbers composing each of these groups – to recipients from both Abifarma (representing primarily joint ventures) and Alanac (representing national firms). I also, of course, sent questionnaires to SEI and CEME. Most university professor recipients were at *Universidade Federal do Rio de Janeiro* (UFRJ) or *Universidade de São Paulo* (USP).

Appendix II
Questionnaire, English version (not sent)

Your answering this questionnaire will be of great assistance to me in completing my doctoral dissertation. It should take only a few moments to complete. You may use the self-addressed, stamped envelope to return it.

ALL INFORMATION WILL BE KEPT STRICTLY CONFIDENTIAL AND ANONYMOUS AND WILL BE USED FOR ACADEMIC PURPOSES ONLY.

Thank you very much!

---

1. gender?

    a. Male

    b. Female

2. Age?

3. With which industry are you affiliated?

4. What is your current position?

5. If you are an *empresário*:

a. Do you own a share of your company?

b. Were you a founder of your company?

c. Did you inherit the company from your family?

6. Educational Level

a. No university study

b. some university study

c. graduate study in Brazil

Universities attended: _____

Field (s) studied: _____

7. How would you describe the socio-economic status of the family in which you grew up?

a. working class

b. middle class

c. upper middle class

d. wealthy

8. Extent of participation in *Diretas Já!* You can choose more than one answer.

a. participated in rallies

b. spoke out publically to persuade others to support it

c. voluntary work

d. financial contributions

e. signed petitions

f. little support of any type

10. How would you describe your political views?

    a. extreme left of center

    b. moderate left

    c. center

    d. moderate right of center

    e. extreme right

11. For which presidential candidate did you vote in the first round of the 1989 elections?

    a. Lula

    b. Collor

    c. Mario Covas

    d. Brizola

    e. Affif

    f. Maluf

    g. Ulysses Guimarães

    h. Other

12. What is your party affiliation?

   a. PMBD

   b. PDS

   c. PSDB

   d. PL

   e. PT

   f. Other

13. What was your party affiliation etc. in 1985?

14. What is the extent of your contact with politicians in the National Congress?

15. Please give your estimate of the number of conferences you attend yearly to discuss political strategy for the industry.

16. Please give your estimate of your total number of articles written to newspapers or other media advocating government support for your industry.

17. Number of interviews given?

18. Computer industry only: do you favor continuation of some form of market reserve policy for your sector?

   a. yes

   b. no

19. Pharmaceutical sector only: what is your position on the new policy recognizing patents for pharmaceutical products?

    a. strongly support

    b. somewhat support

    c. strongly oppose

    d. somewhat oppose

    e. indifferent

20. (OPTIONAL): Any other comments especially with regard to any political efforts of yours on behalf of your sector?

Notes

1 INTRODUCTION

1 Sanjaya Lall (1992:185) defines "national technological capabilities" as consisting of physical investment (plant and equipment as well as financial resources), human capital (skills), and technological effort ("efforts by productive enterprises to assimilate and improve upon the relevant technology").

2 Some might argue that, analytically, the computer industry should not be linked so strongly to national security concerns, and that there is nothing particularly "social" about the pharmaceutical industry. But in Brazil, as elsewhere in Latin America, there was a strong basis for these claims.

Clearly, development of a national computer industry can be seen as important to civilian as well as military regimes. Aside from enhancing national security, such development might also bring about a variety of spin-off industries, and, after all, access to computers is vital to all nations attempting to modernize their productive sectors and compete internationally. For these reasons, the civilians' actually *increasing* support for the military's computer policy might not seem all that surprising.

In the context of 1980s Brazil, however, this outcome was surprising indeed. As the process of *abertura*, or "opening" of the political system progressed, opposition politicians were becoming increasingly outspoken in their criticism of policies linked to the military regime. The military's computer policy was certainly not immune to this criticism. Moreover, during the course of the 1980s, the objective, purely technocratic rationale for pursuing the policy was beginning to wane. Despite the democratic opposition's early (and perhaps misguided) fears, even the military's strong support for the computer industry was beginning to decline.

With regard to the national pharmaceutical industry, it *was* linked to the social welfare of the population, at least in the minds of policymakers in Brazil. This linkage had a relatively long tradition in Brazil, going back at least as far as the early 1960s, when strong nationalist sentiment was sweeping the country. At that time, outrage among politicians and others over foreign dominance of the pharmaceutical sector, and the resultant high prices for medications (which put an excessive burden on the poor), was strong and widespread. The tradition has continued to the present, as high prices for imported medicine, as well as the practice of "self-medication" (obtaining medications directly from local pharmacies under guidance from the pharmacist, without the intermediary and costly step of obtaining a doctor's prescription) persist.

3 Despite President Collor's firm commitment to liberalize the Brazilian economy, he was able only to bring about a gradual – and even then only partial – phasing out of the computer market reserve. In the pharmaceutical sector, on the other hand, all potential proposals for any sort of market reserve were quickly eliminated from political discourse. Not only that, but the one relatively narrow goal that those in the pharmaceutical sector had managed to articulate and lobby for with some fervor, the non-recognition of patents on pharmaceutical products, was quickly overturned.

4 In Portuguese, *corpo técnico* means literally "technical corps," and refers usually to technically trained personnel working within a company, government ministry, or other agency. In this dissertation, I have adopted the term but have expanded significantly on its meaning.

5 I define "political affinity" as the extent of similarity between the political characteristics of a given industry's *corpo técnico* and a dominant political coalition or party. One aspect of political affinity is the ability of the *corpo técnico* to influence policymakers. Another is the degree to which *corpo técnico* members are willing to participate in and support particular industrial programs that are seen as serving the interests of the dominant coalition or party. One or both aspects of political affinity played an important role in the cases examined here.

The phrase "political affinity" itself is derivative of "elective affinity," a term once used in chemistry to describe the strong attraction some substances exhibit for one another that may make them combine readily under certain circumstances. Goethe borrowed the term to describe human love relationships in his novel, *Elective Affinities*. Much later, Guillermo O'Donnell borrowed it from Goethe in his 1973 book *Modernization and Bureaucratic-Authoritarianism*, to describe the association between economic "deepening" and authoritarian coups in Latin America. Thus, while the term "political affinity" may have even earlier antecedents than O'Donnell's use of "elective affinity," one can argue that it does have some resonance within the literature on Latin American politics.

6 The *Partido do Movimento Democrático* Brasileiro (PMDB) was the main civilian opposition party in Brazil during the time leading up to the transition. Even in the closing years of the military regime, the PMDB, as the party "on the rise," was in the process of becoming the dominant actor on the Brazilian political scene. And although the first president actually to take office after the transition, José Sarney, was himself a member of the conservative PFL party, Tancredo Neves – the president elected in the indirect 1985 election that brought about the transition – had been a member of the PMDB, and most of the key cabinet ministers in the new government were members of that party. (Tancredo died shortly after his election, and Sarney, as his Vice President, took over.)

7 Government policies can be important but rarely (if ever) the only factors in determining economic outcomes. "Economic outcomes" refers to the economic consequences of government policies in the computer and pharmaceutical sectors: i.e., the number of domestic firms created and the revenues generated from the industry.

8 In precise terms, the "market reserve" was the set of protectionist policies, established informally during the late 1970s and passed officially into law by the National Congress in 1984, which banned importation into Brazil of foreign personal computers and other related products.

9 Chapter 4 will discuss this subject in much greater detail.

10 Important critiques of the dependency perspective include Bill Warren's *Imperialism: Pioneer of Capitalism* (London: New Left Books, 1980); Sanjaya Lall, "Is 'Dependence' a Useful Concept in Analysing Underdevelopment?", *World Development* 3 (November-December 1975), pp. 799–810; and Robert Packenham, *The Dependency Movement* (Cambridge: Harvard University Press, 1992).

11 One way in which the "bargaining" school differs from the dependency approach is that it argues that less-developed countries actually can transcend dependence on a permanent basis, at least in some areas. A classic example of this approach is Theodore Moran's *Multinational Corporations and the Politics of Dependence: Copper in Chile* (Princeton: Princeton University Press, 1974). Some studies, such as Peter Evan's *Dependent Development* (1979), employ a combination of the two approaches.

12 Emanuel Adler, *The Power of Ideology: The Quest for Technological Autonomy in Argentina and Brazil* (Berkeley: University of California Press, 1987). Adler also tries to use this argument to explain the relative "success" or "failure" of other industries in Brazil and Argentina. However, serious difficulties can arise in attempting to use political or ideological explanations to account for a phenomenon as complex, and with as many causes, as economic "success." This book, therefore, uses political explanations to explain *political* (policy) outcomes. Chapter 5 then goes on to make the argument that policies can have an important impact on economic outcomes.

13 To repeat, the *corpo técnico* consists of more than just Adler's *"técnicos"*; it is a broadly based coalition of businessmen, scientists, and technically trained government bureaucrats.

14 See Frederic C. Deyo (ed.), *The Political Economy of the New Asian Industrialism* (Ithaca: Cornell University Press, 1987). In these cases the governments discussed tend to have the capacity, when needed, to protect indigenous infant industries from the rigors of competition with the transnationals, until the industries can compete on their own.

15 Of course, many of these people were extremely well-read and were familiar with the writings of Peter Evans, Emanuel Adler, etc. To what extent their opinions were influenced by their readings of these authors is a disturbing question. On the other hand, given these individuals' direct involvement with the industries in question, they were not likely to take seriously for long any explanation that was too far removed from reality.

16 At the very least, in terms of human capital.

17 Guillermo O'Donnell, *Modernization and Bureaucratic-Authoritarianism: Studies in South American Politics* (Institute of International Studies, University of California, Berkeley, 1973). Although O'Donnell's theory has come under heavy criticism, his discussion of key social actors within BA regimes is still useful for our purposes here.

18 O'Donnell elaborates on the concept of perceived "threat" to the socioeconomic order, which is the military's pretext for intervention, in "Tensions in the Bureaucratic-Authoritarian State," in David Collier (ed.), *The New Authoritarianism in Latin America* (Princeton: Princeton University Press, 1979), pp. 285–316.

19 During a military regime, the military (air force, army, navy) can be described, in Alfred Stepan's terms, as both the military as government (the top leadership, who direct the government) and the military as institution (this constitutes most

of the military organization, including the staff on the bases, the military bureaucracy and the reserves). Thus, during the authoritarian period in Brazil one component of the military formed the government and another component, the military as institution, acted as a highly favored social group. See Alfred Stepan, *Rethinking Military Politics: Brazil and the Southern Cone* (Princeton: Princeton University Press, 1988).

20 Indeed, those lobbying for greater government support for the national pharmaceutical sector made such arguments frequently during the military years.

21 Stepan's arguments support the view that the Brazilian military saw the national computer industry as vital to its own interests. See Alfred Stepan, *Rethinking*, p. 57.

22 This is the term Schmitter uses in "Still the Century of Corporatism?" (*Review of Politics* 36, 1974, pp. 61–85), to distinguish the variety of corporatism linked with many authoritarian regimes from the variety ("societal corporatism") associated with some pluralist democracies.
Alfred Stepan carries this distinction one step further with his highly theoretical analysis of different kinds of corporatism in Latin America in *State and Society in Peru* (Princeton: Princeton University Press, 1978). This view places Mexico's mobilized kind of polity at one extreme analytically (the "inclusionary" pole) and Brazil's harsh authoritarianism under military rule at another (the "exclusionary" pole). For our purposes Schmitter's distinction is sufficient.

23 Chapters 2 and 3 will discuss these outcomes in greater detail. Also, we must emphasize again that this book does *not* attempt to analyze the relative "success" and "failure" of the two industries; this phenomenon is too complex to investigate here in all of its economic, financial and technological aspects. Thus, the focus of our analysis is on a *political* variable, the level of government political support for a given industry. After all, one reasonably can argue, as does this book (see Chapter 5), that the level of government political support for a particular industry is a central factor in determining the extent of that industry's eventual success or failure. And the difference in levels of government support for the Brazilian computer and pharmaceutical industries is sharp indeed.

24 Nevertheless, in order to understand what happened later, Chapters 2 and 3 do offer some brief discussion of previous events.

25 Members of the National Congress.

26 Interview with Senator Severo Gomes, Brasilia, December 5, 1989.

27 Although the National Congress worked out an accord in June, 1991, to relax some aspects of the market reserve, important restrictions on foreign participation (discussed in more detail in Chapter 2) remained until 1992.

2 THE COMPUTER INDUSTRY

1 *Tecnicos* is the Portuguese word used most often to refer to technically trained government bureaucrats. *Empresários* are business owners. I use this term to refer to owners of national firms (not TNCs).

2 Chapter 4 will discuss the political orientation of these individuals in detail.

3 For documentation on the differences between the three branches of the Brazilian Armed Forces, and on how these differences affected their actions, see Wendy Hunter, "Back to the Barracks? The Military in Post-authoritarian Brazil," Ph.D. dissertation, Department of Political Science, U.C. Berkeley, 1992.

4 Dantas, p. 46. In this particular case, given the particular nature of Saur's colleague, things did not turn out so badly after all.

5 See *ibid.*, pp. 38–56.

6 Interview with Edson Fregni, President of Scopus Computers, São Paulo, December, 1989.

7 We should point out, of course, that we are speaking of the computer *corpo técnico* as a general group; naturally, there were exceptions to this general trend. But Edson Fregni himself, at the time he won the Engineer of the Year award, was only 35 years old.

8 Again, this is Adler's argument, which is summarized in Chapter 1.

9 Chamber of Deputies, the lower house of the Brazilian National Congress (the upper house is the Senate). Members of the *Câmara dos Deputados* are called *deputados*.

10 In Portuguese, "informática" is the broad term that encompasses just about anything to do with the computer industry. For example, computer products are "informática." I sometimes use the English equivalent, "informatics."

11 Dantas, p. 257. As Dantas reports, both *deputados* were noted for their work during the military regime as strong defenders of the rights of political prisoners.

12 *Ibid.*

13 Seligman's career trajectory illustrates the pattern common among members of the computer *corpo técnico*. That is, his specialized technical training enabled him to transfer his skills from one kind of job to another with relative ease. Having started out as an electrical engineer, he became Secretary General of the Pedroso Horta Foundation, the PMDB's think-tank in Brasilia, in 1981. Thus, for most of the duration of his activities described here, he could be classified as a *técnico*. Recently, however, Seligman began his own computer firm and became an *empresário* (national business owner). The pervasiveness of this kind of flow from one branch of the computer *corpo técnico* to another seemed to help it, in contrast to the pharmaceutical *corpo técnico*, remain cohesive and unified in its policies and approach.

14 Interview with Milton Seligman, Brasilia, November 25, 1989.

15 *Ibid.*; also, interview with *deputada* Cristina Tavares, Brasilia, October 2, 1989.

16 The extent to which Fruet trusted Seligman and other members of the computer *corpo técnico* became clear when I tried to make an appointment to see him. After I had made several calls to Fruet's office, one of his staff members urged me to speak with Seligman or Fernando Calicchio, current President of the *corpo técnico*'s main lobbying organization, *Movimento Brasil de Informática* (MBI). As the staff member explained, "the *deputado* told me to tell you that you might as well speak with Seligman or Calicchio, because their views on *informatica* are identical with his. Anything they tell you about the subject is the same thing the *deputado* will tell you."

17 Interview with Milton Seligman, Brasilia, November 25, 1989; interview with Cristina Tavares, Brasilia, October 2, 1989, and December 5, 1989.

18 Further evidence of the similarity of their views, and the closeness of their working relationship, was their collaboration on a book about the informatics policy and the importance of the *Lei de Informática* to Brazil's development. See Cristina Tavares and Milton Seligman, *Informática: A Batalha do Seculo XII* (Rio de Janeiro: Paz e Terra, 1984).

19 Interview with Fernando Calicchio, President, *Movimento Brasil de Informática*, Brasilia, November 24, 1989.

20 Tavares, with Seligman's help and that of other *corpo técnico* members, was responsible for the National Congress's initiatives to institutionalize the government's policy in this area, a policy which previously had been handed down by executive decrees and was therefore subject to the whims of the government in power at the time.

21 Edson Fregni, Fernando Calicchio, Ricardo Saur, Artur Pereira Nunes, and Claudio Mammana, among others – all businessmen or technically trained people working within the sector.

22 Quoted in Dantas, p. 260. (My translation.) This was the view of the General Secretary of the Brazilian National Security Council. The source of the quotation is somewhat surprising, given that this is not the usual job title of someone (a military general to boot) concerned with democratic niceties.

23 See Chapter 4.

24 Interview with Edson Fregni, President of Scopus Computers, São Paulo, December, 1989.

25 *Ibid.*

26 While the other two components of the *corpo técnico*, *técnicos* (technocrats, i.e., technically trained bureaucrats) and university professors, played lesser roles in winning government support for particular policies at the time period discussed here than did the *empresários*, they were important nevertheless. The *técnicos*, of course, had played a crucial part in the early phase of the government's program, before the *empresários* existed in any significant numbers, and continued to be key players (e.g., Milton Seligman) at this phase of the computer program. *Técnicos* from the *Secretaria Especial de Informática* (SEI), of course, were forceful supporters of the program, although, at least in the waning years of the military regime, some PMDB members in the National Congress were not comfortable with them. University professors such as Paulo Bastos Tigre, industrial economist at the Universidade Federal do Rio de Janeiro (UFRJ), himself former vice president for planning at SEI, aided the *corpo técnico*'s cause with data-laden books explaining the importance of the *Lei de Informática* and evaluating its success. And in contrast with their counterparts in the pharmaceutical *corpo técnico*, the *técnicos* and university professors in the computer *corpo técnico* seemed to be more or less in agreement with each other and with the *empresários* about what the nature of the government's policy toward the computer sector should be.

27 Members of the National Congress.

28 The Figuereido Administration's version was much more favorable to the multinational corporations. It permitted joint ventures and put fewer restrictions on computer imports.

29 *Veja* magazine provided an account of this event somewhat later in "Confusão Electrônica," *Veja*, (July 16, 1986).

30 Dantas gives Milton Seligman primary credit for this idea (p. 274).

31 Some might find it odd that Sarney, originally from the right-of-center military-affiliated PDS party, would be so supportive of a policy for which the left-of-center computer *corpo técnico* was lobbying so strenuously and which had such strong support from members of the PMDB. It is important to remember, however, that Sarney was in a weak and vulnerable position in the PMDB party by virtue of the way he ascended to the office of president. (Sarney had been vice-president until the elected president, Tancredo Neves, died shortly before he

could be inagurated.) Given the PMDB's – and Tancredo's – strong support for the computer policy, Sarney was in no position to oppose it.

32 When the Foreign Minister made some comments suggesting a willingness to negotiate about Brazil's policy, the Minister of Science and Technology said, with some irritation, "I won't discuss that. The Informatics Law is untouchable, as President Sarney has determined, and it can only be modified by the National Congress." ("'A lei é intocavel,' afirma Renato Archer," *Gazeta Mercantil*, May 5, 1986.)

33 Interview with Luciano Coutinho, ex-Secretary-General of the MCT, São Paulo, December 14, 1989. In a way, Coutinho, with a Ph.D. in economics from Cornell University, was himself a member of the *corpo técnico*.

34 Ironically, Collor himself was impeached in 1992 for diversion of government funds for his own use.

35 Although the market reserve was finally eliminated in 1992, tariffs on imported computers remain at a relatively high level of 35 percent.

3 THE PHARMACEUTICAL INDUSTRY

1 In part, as noted in Chapter 1 and as will become more evident later in this chapter, this had to do with a low degree of access for this industry.

2 *Comissão Parlamentar Inquérito, Câmara dos Deputados*, Brasilia, 1980.

3 Interview with Roberto Pereira, economic advisor and Vice President of CEME, May 4, 1989.

4 When I asked the former Minister of Social Welfare, Jarbas Passarinho – supposedly the man with ultimate responsibility for Scardua's dismissal – about these events, he could not remember details. I believe that the poor memory of Passarinho, a passionate supporter of the military and a senator elected as a candidate of the military-related PDS party at the time of my interview with him (and currently Brazil's Minister of Justice), was genuine; he indicated that the General-Secretary of the Ministry, Joffre Frejat, had been in charge of such day-to-day affairs. This official, who at the time of my interview with him was a *deputado* elected on the conservative "Frente Liberal" (PFL) party's ticket, was much more aware of the past events but skirted the issue at hand, suggesting poor financial management of the entire Ministry of Social Welfare before Passarinho came in as the cause of the administrative changes. These changes included the departure of the previous Minister of Social Welfare, Helio Beltrao, who – influenced by Scardua – had been a strong supporter of Profarma. Frejat and Passarinho were not opposed to the Profarma *per se*, Frejat explained, just to promoting such a program when the Ministry was in such financial chaos and Brazil was engaged in negotiations on its foreign debt. (Interview with Jarbas Passarinho, Brasilia, August 2, 1989; interview with Joffre Frejat, Brasilia, August 3, 1989.)

5 Fernando Henrique Cardoso's essay on "bureaucratic rings" provides an analysis of this kind of decisionmaking, the kind that traditionally has prevailed in Brazil.

6 *Matérias primas*, the primary ingredients or raw materials from which finished pharmaceutical products were made, were the primary cause of the Brazilian pharmaceutical industry's negative balance of trade. As will be explained in Chapter 5, in the pharmaceutical industry it was the manufacture of these primary ingredients, rather than the assembling of the final medications, that required highly advanced, sophisticated technology.

7 As a further testament to the relative weakness of the pharmaceutical *corpo técnico* in relation to the transnational corporations, the Minister of Industry and Commerce, one of the five original supporters of the proposal and under whose auspices it had been announced, later denied even that he had signed the document to approve it. This was an astonishing revelation to reporters, who had seen his signature on the proposal and who knew that initially he had been very active in trying to obtain the signatures of the other ministers.

8 See *Revista Brasileira de Tecnológia*, vol. 18, no. 3, 1987.

9 Interview with Kurt Politzer, Brasilia, August 28, 1989.

10 See Politzer's testimony before the Senate Investigating Commission on the Pharmaceutical Industry in *Diario do Senado Federal na Comissão Parlamentar de Inquérito, Reunião* 4, November 22, 1988.

11 Interview with Roberto Pereira, Vice President for Planning at CEME, July 20, 1989. (I had several conversations with Pereira about this issue at different times, as well as with other *técnicos,* empresários, university professors, and even *deputados* and Senators in the National Congress. All described superprofiting in essentially these same terms.)

12 Interview with Dr Zich, in charge of the CDI's "Química Fina" section, Brasilia, August 24, 1989.

13 Interview with Geraldo Giovanni at Unicamp, Campinas, January 5. 1990.

14 Note that this figure includes chemical firms with operations related to the pharmaceutical sector, as well as strictly pharmaceutical companies.

15 As CEME's 1988 annual report stated, "the establishment of the New Republic was received with enormous expectations by CEME" (CEME, *Relatório Anual de Atividades*, 1988, *versão preliminar*, p. 2. (My translation.)

16 Marta Nobrega, President of CEME at this time, suggested this in an interview. (Interview with Marta Nobrega, former president of CEME, Brasilia, May 18, 1989.) In addition, in reading through hundreds of newspaper articles, testimony by *corpo técnico* members in the Constituent Assembly, and informational pamphlets by CEME and other organizations working within the pharmaceutical industry, my strong impression was that with the transition from military to civilian rule, *corpo técnico* members altered the nature of their arguments for government support for technological development in the sector. Whereas before they had emphasized the strategic importance of a strong national pharmaceutical industry, under the New Republic regime they emphasized social aspects more.

17 Interview with Dr Nicia Maria Mourao Henrique, *técnico* in Grupo 3, SDI, Brasilia, May 15, 1989.

18 CEME, *Relatorio*, p. 3. (My translation.) Roberto Pereira noted, however, that this increase came to an end after one year. See Pereira interviews, already cited.

19 Interview with Marta Nobrega, former President of CEME, May 18, 1989; *Lei Ordinaria*, passed by the Constituent Assembly Senate Committee dealing with these matters, 1987.

20 In condensed form, these planks were: (1) that the government would guarantee the installment of pharmaceutical assistance, in the plan for basic attention to health, to all Brazilians; (2) in the sectors of the economy in which technological and industrial autonomy has not attained a degree compatible with the necessities of development of the country, genuinely national companies should be given preferential treatment, in terms of fiscal and financial incentives; (3) acquisitions of pharmaceutical products, for public use, will be from those items produced by national firms, when available (interview with Marta Nobrega; also see *Ministério*

*da Saude/*CEME pamphlet, "Medicamentos Essenciais: Os Caminhos da Autonomia," January, 1987).

21 The newspaper articles "Remédio pode ter reserva," *(Correio Brasiliense,* July 4, 1986) and "O CDI quer reserva de mercado para fabricar matérias-primas," *(Gazeta Mercantil,* July 10, 1986) discuss the market reserve proposals. "EUA não aprovam proposta do MIC;" *(Gazeta Mercantil,* July 14, 1986) reports on the international pressures to prevent them from going into effect.

4 POLITICAL CHARACTERISTICS OF THE *CORPOS TÉCNICOS*

1 For discussion of the survey, and for a copy of the survey itself, see the Appendices. Note that the statistical tests in this chapter are intended merely to complement the in-depth interviews in Chapters 2 and 3. Although the sampling technique was not strictly random, I took care – as explained in the appendices – to make sure the samples were representative. While not indicating strict statistical "significance," then, the statistical tests do indicate that a strong trend exists that supports the overall argument.

2 Percentages have been rounded to the nearest whole number.

3 For the most influential and active computer *corpo técnico* members – as Chapter 2 showed and as we will discuss further below – the percentage was much higher still.

4 Charles Lindblom, *Politics and Markets* (New York: Basic Books, 1977). While the crude instrumental Marxist framework Lindblom uses to analyze this phenomenon is not at all confirmed by the evidence, the book does highlight some of the special resources business firms can call upon to exert political influence.

5 Of course, this difference in the nature of ownership in the two industries resulted primarily from the fact that pharmaceutical firms had been around long enough for them to be passed on to succeeding generations. In the computer industry, of course, *empresários* had to start their own firms. Nevertheless, the distinct political characteristics that resulted from these differences were striking.

6 These percentages have been rounded to the nearest whole number.

7 As noted here, many of the *corpo técnico* members did study at universities in the US; others studied at British and French universities. The predominance of study in the US among many of the key players is primarily a result of the fact that many of the US universities mentioned were major training centers for those interested in computer technology and computer science at this time. My point is that graduate study abroad at good universities (whether they be American or British or French) was correlated with a certain kind of political orientation on the part of the students.

8 These percentages are rounded to the nearest whole number. Because this particular set of comparisons is not binary (includes more than two-by-two categories), we cannot use the chi square test for these figures.

9 Many of the more marginal candidates dropped out as the campaign progressed, and some came in later – indeed, Silvio Santos, a popular variety show host, entered the race just a few weeks before the first-round elections. After immediately taking first place in the polls, however, Santos had to drop out of the race when the Supreme Electoral Court declared his candidacy invalid.

10 While the 1985 presidential election was not direct, as the *Diretas Já!* campaign had demanded, this pro-democratic movement was a key factor in bringing the civilian PMDB candidate to victory.

11 The number of individuals in each of the *corpos técnicos* as a whole – *empresários, técnicos*, and university professors – was approximately 300 to 400 for each industry.

12 One striking observation about the computer *corpo técnico* is that individual members of it seemed able to shift easily from one part (e.g., the *técnicos* segment) to another (e.g., the *empresários*). Indeed, in contrast with the pharmaceutical *corpo técnico*, there was a great deal of shifting about from one branch of the computer *corpo técnico* to another. This fluidity of movement between the different segments may have contributed to the computer *corpo técnico*'s relative unity and cohesion on policy issues.

13 Brazilians have a peculiar manner of addressing people. People are addressed by their first, last, and/or other names depending on which are most unusual and distinctive. Even high officials are occasionally referred to in this way, sometimes along with their titles. Thus José Ezil Veiga da Rocha, for example, former president of SEI, was often referred to as "Ezil Veiga." While sometimes confusing, this method does help one remember names and is easier than reciting the frequently long, multi-syllable Brazilian surnames. When the meaning is very clear, we will sometimes use the same method here.

14 Significantly, many other members of the computer *corpo técnico* studied at ITA: José Doria Porto, Claudio Mammana, Mario and José Ripper, among others. During an interview, Dr José Ripper spoke at great length about the rigors of the institution at that time. He emphasized that the ITA, despite being under the auspices of the Air Force, was run on democratic principles. With increased repression of academic freedoms by the military in the late 1960s, the special ambience of the place, which had nurtured so many future computer *corpo técnico* members, was destroyed (interview with José Ellis Ripper, Campinas, January, 1990).

15 Along with Milton Seligman, discussed in Chapter 2.

16 Telephone conversation with Antonio Gaspar, Brasilia, 1989.

17 In the second, run-off round, Pereira voted for Luis Ignacio "Lula" da Silva, of the Worker's Party, who lost to Fernando Collor. Both Roberto Freire (the Communist Party candidate) and Lula were in favor of continuation of non-recognition of patents, as well as increased funding for the pharmaceutical sector.

18 Interview with Roberto Pereira, Brasilia, 1989.

19 In fact, disillusionment with the PMDB was a phenomenon common throughout Brazil after the 1986 congressional elections. Soon after taking office in 1985, President Sarney and the PMDB in Congress had implemented a program known as the Cruzado Plan, which dealt with inflation by imposing strict government control on prices. In addition to the inevitable economic problems inherent in such a policy, the Cruzado Plan created a short-lived euphoria among the Brazilian population. This turned into bitter disillusionment toward Sarney in particular and the PMDB itself when the Plan was rescinded immediately after the PMDB won an overwhelming majority in the 1986 elections.

20 See testimony before the *Senado Federal Comissão Parlamentar Sobre A Indústria Farmacêutica*, Brasilia, 1988.

21 Interview with Kurt Politzer, Brasilia, 1989.

22 *Ibid.*

23 *Ibid.*

24 Interview with Geraldo Giovanni, Unicamp, January 5, 1990.

25 The great majority of members of the Senate Investigating Commission on the

Pharmaceutical Industry, established in 1988, were affiliated with the PMDB. Hence, they were at least potentially susceptible to the kind of lobbying campaigns the computer *corpo técnico* waged on the Chamber of Deputies Commission on Science, Technology, and Informatics. Yet, the Senator and PMDB member who was chair of this Commission certainly made no effort to refer the researcher to "advisers" in the pharmaceutical *corpo técnico*, who would be able to explain his views as well as he could (interview with Senator Leite Chaves, Brasilia, 1989). Indeed, minutes of the initial hearings of the Commission indicate that the Senators themselves had to suggest names for expert witnesses to the Commission's hearings – and they seemed to have a difficult time of thinking of many (Senate Hearings on the Investigating Commission on the Pharmaceutical Industry, 1988).

5 THE OTHER VARIABLES IN THE MODEL

1 Hubert Schmitz and José Cassiolato, "Fostering Hi-Tech Industries in Developing Countries: Introduction," in Hubert Schmitz and José Cassiolato (eds.), *Hi-Tech For Industrial Development* (London: Routledge, 1992), pp. 1–20, summarize this approach and show how it can be applied to the developing countries in general, and in particular to the Brazilian computer industry. A thoughtful and interesting application of this approach to the Brazilian telecommunications industry is Michael Hobday's *Telecommunications in Developing Countries: The Challenge From Brazil* (London: Routledge, 1990).

2 The neoliberal "product cycle" theory, of course, would hold just the opposite view.

3 A sales executive in Brazil with the US-based TNC, UpJohn Pharmaceuticals, told me that his firm saw great potential for profit in the Brazilian market for a new anti-baldness drug. At the time of my conversation with this executive (April, 1989), his firm was launching a campaign to market this product in Brazil along with an anti-wrinkle cream. Such products would never appear on the Rename list.

4 During a number of panel discussions on future policy for the industry at the 1989 *Feira de Informática*, held in São Paulo, speakers repeatedly cited this concern, as did *corpo técnico* members at 1989 meetings of the Science and Technology Commission in the *Câmara dos Deputados*, Brasilia.

5 "Articulation" and "disarticulacion" (*articulação* and *disarticulação*) were the words computer *corpo técnico* members virtually always used when referring to this issue.

6 "SUMOC" was the name of a particular kind of law dealing with monetary policy; 113 was the number of this specific law.

7 Also, per capita consumption of medications in this seventh-largest market was 18th in the world. (Abifarma, "A indústria farmacêutica no Brasil: a realidade," information pamphlet, 1988, p. 23.) This was a dismal indicator of Brazil's lack of regard for social welfare during the long military years.

8 For details, see Carlos Osmar Bertero, "Drugs and Dependency in Brazil – An Empirical Study of Dependency Theory: The Case of the Pharmaceutical Industry" (Ph.D. dissertation, Graduate School of Management, Cornell University, 1972).

9 For more about Codotec and its involvement in the pharmaceutical industry, see

Laerte Rimoli, "Caminhos para a auto-suficiencia," *Revista Brasileira de Tecnológia*, Vol. 18, No. 3 (March, 1987), pp. 7–14.

10 This Ministry was demoted, for a time, from its status as a ministry in the late 1980s, only to be reinstated again later. Severo Gomes, a prominent senator in the PMDB party who had been Minister of Industry and Commerce during the military regime, told me that pressures on President Sarney from the foreign economic interests had caused this occurrence, because the Ministry's *técnicos* were too supportive of development of domestic technological capabilities in Brazil (interview with Senator Severo Gomes, Brasilia, December 5, 1989).

11 Cibran accomplished these feats under the guidance of Executive Director Adilson Xavier, for many years highly active President of the national industry's lobbying organization, Alanac. Xavier's father, Osmar, also a high-level executive in Cibran had been one of Alanac's founders.

12 In Charles Lindblom's sense of the term, as explained in his classic article on public policy, "The science of 'muddling through,'" *Public Administration Review*, 1959.

6 APPLICATION OF THE ARGUMENT TO OTHER CASES

1 As explained in Chapter 1, the definition of "high-technology" industries used in this volume is those industries characterized by rapid technological innovation and high expenditure on R&D.

2 With the exception of the South Korean cases – an anomaly to be discussed more fully in the conclusion.

3 Analysis of the role of scientists and others with advanced technical training is particularly relevant to the newly industrializing countries. In the NICs such individuals – where the access and political affinity variables permit – tend, as members of the relatively small, highly educated elite, to have far more political influence than their counterparts in the industrialized nations.

4 While "nuclear scientists," i.e., physicists and engineers with specialized nuclear training, were few in Brazil, they tended strongly to oppose the military regime's programs in this area. They were supported in their views by Brazilian physicists and engineers as a whole.

5 We do not examine the Indian case here because that country was not undergoing a process of democratization during the period of the nuclear industry's development.

6 This article referred to Goldemberg as one of a number of "left-of-center" young "progressives" that Montoro was appointing to fill important jobs in his administration.

7 Significantly, José Goldemberg, a highly respected nuclear physicist and active opponent of the military's nuclear program, had been President of the SBPC the year before.

8 As noted, the complete "nuclear fuel cycle," which included the ability to reprocess or enrich uranium, was an important component in the indigenous manufacture of nuclear weapons.

9 Such as it was – hose physicists, engineers, technicians, and *empresários* with technical expertise in the nuclear industry. But also influential in this sector, as already noted, was the larger body of technically trained physicists and engineers who concerned themselves with the nuclear industry, members of such

associations as the Brazilian Society for the Advancement of Science (SBPC) and the Society of Brazilian Physicists (SBF).

10 By the late 1970s, censorship had lessened sufficiently for such public debate to take place.

11 Note that throughout this book, "government political support for" a given industry refers to government political support for *national*, indigenous industry, not for foreign industry operating inside national borders.

12 Adler quotes Poneman as supporting his own argument of the importance of the "non-partisan" agency.

13 In fact, Iraoloagoitia's being from the *Navy* may have influenced his ready willingness to go along with Peron's instructions on completely merit-based, non-partisan hiring. As will be explained further below, the Navy, as a branch of the military, tends to have a different political orientation than the more conservative, hardline elements (the Army). For more on this argument, see Wendy Hunter, "Back to the barracks? The military in post-authoritarian Brazil,"(Ph.D. dissertation, Department of Political Science, University of California, Berkeley, 1992).

14 The AERI program and overseas training had developed far less than the thousands needed.

15 While the advent of democratic government may change this situation somewhat, the authoritarian aspect of policymaking in South Korea (to be discussed in the next chapter) is unlikely to change very much.

7 CONCLUSION

1 This solution would only be useful in selected instances; if applied indiscriminately to many sectors, the result could be excessive policy fragmentation and chaos.

Bibliography

"A lei é intocável." afirma Renato Archer (May 5, 1986) *Gazeta Mercantil.*

Abicomp (1989) "Informatica Brasil: a informática brasileira depois da Nova República." São Paulo: Editora Política.

"ABIF da apoio à iniciativa de Medici." (June 30, 1971) *O Estado de São Paulo.*

Abifarma (1988) "A indústria farmacêutica no Brasil: a realidade." Informational pamphlet.

Abranches, Sergio (1976) "The divided Leviathan." Ph.D. dissertation, Government Department, Cornell University.

Adler, Emanuel (1987) *The Power of Ideology: The Quest for Technological Autonomy in Argentina and Brazil.* Berkeley: University of California Press.

Amsden, Alice (1989) *Asia's Next Giant.* Oxford: Oxford University Press.

Baloyra, Enrique (ed.)(1987) *Comparing New Democracies: Transition and Consolidation in Mediterranean Europe and the Southern Cone.* Boulder and London: Westview Press.

Barberio, José Carlos (August 5, 1983) "A Ceme e a indústria químicofarmacêutica nacional." *Estado de São Paulo.*

Bates, Robert (March 1991) "The economics of transitions to democracy," *PS:Political Science and Politics.* pp. 26–7.

Bennett, D., and Sharpe, K. (1985) *The State v. the Multinationals: The Case of the Mexican Automobile Industry.* Princeton: Princeton University Press.

Bennett, Douglas (1979) "Transnational corporations and the political economy of export promotion: the case of the Mexican automobile industry." *International Organization*, Vol. 33.

Bertero, Carlos Osmar (1972) "Drugs and dependency in Brazil – an empirical case study of dependency theory: the case of the pharmaceutical industry." Ph.D. dissertation, School of Management, Cornell University.

"Brazil: why nuclear power may be losing its appeal." (July 20, 1981) *Business Week.*

Bunge, Federica M. (1982) *South Korea: A Country Study.* Washington D.C.: Foreign Area Studies, The American University.

Carvalho, Joaquim de (1987) "O Acordo Nuclear Brasil-Alemanha." In Carvalho (ed.), *O Brasil Nuclear.* Porto Alegre: Tche Editora, Ltda.

Cassiolato, José E. (1992) "The user–producer connection in hi-tech." In Hubert Schmitz and José Cassiolato (eds), *Hi-Tech For Industrial Development*, London: Routledge.

Ceme (1988) "*Relatório Anual de Atividades.*" versão preliminar, Brasilia: Internal Ceme document.

"Collor's nuclear disclosure sets off alarm bells." (November 29, 1990) *Latin American Regional Reports: Brazil.* London: Latin American Newsletters, Ltd.

"Confusão eletrônica." (July 16, 1986) *Veja.*

"Controvérsia sobre informática dificulta negociaçôes com EUA." (June 29, 1986) *Jornal do Brasil.*

"Crescem as pressões contra o programa de apoio ã indústria nacional." (June 22, 1983) *Folha de São Paulo.*

Dantas, Vera (1988) *Guerrilha Tecnológica: A Verdadeira História da Política Nacional da Informática.* Rio de Janeiro: Livros Técnicos e Cientifícos Editora, Ltda.

Deyo, Frederic C. (ed.) (1987) *The Political Economy of the New Asian Industrialism.* Ithaca: Cornell University Press.

Dietz, James L. (1990) "Technological autonomy, linkages, and development." In James L. Dietz and Dilmus D. James (eds), *Progress Toward Development in Latin America*, Boulder and London: Lynne Rienner.

The Economist Intelligence Unit (1985) Quarterly Economic Report: Brazil, Annual Supplement.

Enos, J.L. (1991) *The Creation of Technological Capability in Developing Countries*, London: Pinter.

"EUA não aprovam proposta do MIC." (July 14, 1986) *Gazeta Mercantil.*

Evans, Peter (1979) *Dependent Development: The Alliance of State, Multinational, and Local Capital in Brazil.* Princeton: Princeton University Press.

—— (1986) "State, capital, and the transformation of dependence: the Brazilian case." *World Development*, Vol. 14, No. 7.

—— (1987) "Class, state, and dependence in East Asia: lessons for Latin Americanists." In Frederic Deyo (ed.) *The Political Economy of the New Asian Industrialism.* Ithaca: Cornell University Press.

Fernando Henrique Cardoso (1973) "Associated-dependent development: theoretical and practical implications." In Alfred Stepan (ed.) *Authoritarian Brazil: Origins, Policies, and Future.* New Haven and London: Yale University Press.

Ferraz, João Carlos (May 1988) "A demanda tecnológica da indústria química fina: implicações para política setorial." Texto para discussão No. 168, IEI/UFRJ, May, 1988.

Frank, Andre Gunder (1967) *Capitalism and Underdevelopment in Latin America: Historical Studies in Chile and Brazil.*, New York: Monthly Review Press.

Fregni, Edson (1985) "Lei de Informática: Instrumento de Afirmação Nacional." In Editora Hucitec *A Informática e a Nova República.* São Paulo: Editora Huatec.

"Galveas assina plano de insumos." (September 28, 1983) *Gazeta Mercantil.*

Gereffi, Gary (1978) "Drug firms and dependency in Mexico: the case of the steroid hormone industry." *International Organization*, Vol. 32, No. 1.

—— (1983) *The Pharmaceutical Industry and Dependency in the Third World.* Princeton, N.J.: Princeton University Press.

Gerez, J., and Pedrosa D., (March 1987) "Produção de fármacos, questão de sobrevivência." *Revista Brasileira de Tecnológia*, Vol. 18, No. 3.

Giovanni, Geraldo (July 13, 1987) "É preciso renacionalizar." *O Globo.*

Girotti, Carlos A. (1984) *Estado Nuclear No Brasil.* São Paulo: Editora Brasiliense.

Government of the Republic of Korea (1983) *Fifth Five-year Economic Plan, Revised.*

Grieco, Joseph (1984) *Between Dependency and Autonomy: India's Experience with the International Computer Industry.* Berkeley: University of California Press.

Guimarães, Ulysses (1985) Preface to Editora Hucitec, *A Informática e a Nova República*. São Paulo: Editora Hucitec.

Ha, Yung-Soon (1983) *Nuclear Proliferation, World Order and Korea*. Seoul: Seoul National University Press.

Helena, Sílvia (1980) "A Indústria de computadores: evolução das decisões governmentais." *Revista da Administração Publica*, Vol 14, No. 4.

Hewitt, T. (1992) "Employment and skills in the Brazilian electronics industry." In Hubert Schmitz and José Cassiolato (eds) *Hi-tech For Industrial Development*. London: Routledge.

Hobday, Michael (1990) *Telecommunications in Developing Countries: The Challenge From Brazil*, London: Routledge.

Hunter, Wendy "Back to the barracks? The military in post-authoritarian Brazil." Ph.D. dissertation in progress, Department of Political Science, University of California, Berkeley.

"Indústria farmacêutica tem ultimato." (December 9, 1982) *Jornal de Brasília*.

"Indústria farmacêutica nacional faz associação." (June 3, 1983) *O Estado de São Paulo*.

"Indústria de remédios reduz suas importações." (December 9, 1982) *Estado de São Paulo*.

Johnson, Chalmers "Political institutions and economic performance: the government–busines relationship in Japan, South Korea, and Taiwan." In Deyo *The Political Economy of the New Asian Industrialism*. Ithaca: Cornell University Press.

Jones, L.P., and I. Sakong (n.d.) "Government, business and entrepreneurship in economic development: the Korean case." Harvard University Council on East Asian Studies, *Harvard East Asian Monographs*, No. 91.

Katz, James and Onkar Marwah (eds) (1982) *Nuclear Power in Developing Countries*. Lexington, Mass.: Lexington Books.

Kupfert, David (March 1985) "O Setor de medicamentos no Brasil: aspectos da estructura industrial." UFRJ/IEI Seires. Rio de Janeiro: Universidade Federal de Rio de Janeiro/Instituto de Economia Industrial.

Kwack, Yoon-Chick (1986) "The economic development of Korea, 1965–81." In Yoon Chick Kwack (ed.) *Economic Development In Korea and Taiwan*.

Lall, Sanjaya (1992) "The role of technology in economic development." In Simon Teitel (ed.) *Towards A New Development Strategy For Latin America*, Washington, D.C.: Inter-American Development Bank.

Latin American Development Bank (1988) "Economic and Social Progress in Latin America – 1988 Report".

Lei Ordinária (1987) Constituent Assembly Senate Committee, Brasilia.

Leite, Rogerio Cezar Cerqueira de "Nucleopatas e sofistas." In Carvalho (ed.) *O Brasil Nuclear*. Porto Alegre: Tche Editora, Ltda.

Levine, Daniel (April 1988) "Paradigm lost: dependence to democracy." *Comparative Politics*, Vol. 15, No. 3.

Lindblom, Charles (1959) "The science of 'muddling through.'" *Public Administration Review*.

—— (1977) *Politics and Markets*. New York: Basic Books.

Linz, Juan (1975) "Totalitarian and authoritarian regimes." In Fred I. Greenstein and Nelson W. Polsby (eds), *Handbook For Political Science, Volume 3: Macropolitical Theory*. Reading, Mass.: Addison-Wesley Publishing Company.

Lowi, Theodore (1968) *The End of Liberalism*. Chicago: University of Chicago Press.

136 Bibliography

Leudde-Neurath, Richard (1988) "State intervention and export-oriented development in South Korea." In G. White (ed.) *Developmental States in East Asia*. Sussex, England: Macmillan.

Mainwaring, S., O'Donnell, G., Valenzuela, J.S. (1992) *Issues in Democratic Consolidation*. University of Notre Dame Press.

Mariscotti, Mario (1985) *El Secreto Atómico de Huemel*. Buenos Aires: Sudamericana/Planeta Editores, S.A.

Ministério da Saúde/CEME pamphlet (January 1987) "Medicamentos essenciais: os caminhos da autonomia."

Mirow, Kurt (1979) *Loucura Nuclear: Os Enganos do Acordo Brasil-Alemanha*. Rio de Janeiro: Editora Civilização Brasileira, S.A.

"Montoro opts for young progressives." (January 14, 1983) *Latin America Weekly Report*.

Moran, Theodore (1974) *Multinational Corporations and the Politics of Dependence: Copper in Chile*. Princeton: Princeton University Press.

"Mudança da indústria farmacêutica ainda enfrenta resistência." (May 8, 1983) *O Estado de São Paulo*.

Myers, David J. (1984) "Brazil: reluctant pursuit of the nuclear option," *Orbis*, Winter.

"O CDI quer reserva de mercado para fabricar matérias-primas." (July 10, 1986) *Gazeta Mercantil*.

"O modelo em discussão." (August, 1987) *Info*.

O'Donnell, Guillermo (1973) *Modernization and Bureaucratic-Authoritarianism: Studies in South American Politics*, Institute of International Studies, University of California, Berkeley.

—— (1979) "Tensions in the bureaucratic-authoritarian state." In David Collier (ed.) *The New Authoritarianism in Latin America*. Princeton: Princeton University Press.

O'Donnell, G., Schmitter, P., and Whitehead, L. (eds.) (1986) *Transitions From Authoritarian Rule: Prospects For Democracy*, Volumes 1–4. Baltimore: Johns Hopkins University Press.

"Participação de multinacionais preocupa professores de Unicamp." (June 27, 1983) *O Globo*.

Pereira, Luiz Carlos Bresser (forthcoming) "The crisis of the state approach to Latin America." Chapter 1 in *Economic Crisis and The State in Brazil*, Boulder: Lynne Rienner.

Pereira, Roberto da Costa (1989) "A Central de Medicamentos e a questão dos medicamentos essenciais no Brasil: análise crítica e proposicoes." Unpublished CEME document.

Polanyi, Karl (1944) *The Great Transformation*. Boston: Beacon Press.

Poneman, Daniel (1982) *Nuclear Power in the Developing World*. London: George Allen & Unwin.

"Presidente da Ceme evita imprensa." (June 1984) *Estado de São Paulo*.

"Remédio pode ter reserva." (July 4, 1986) *Correio Brasiliense*.

Rhee, Y. W., Ross-Larson B., and Pursell G. (1984) *Korea's Competitive Edge: Managing The Entry Into World Markets*. Baltimore and London: The Johns Hopkins University Press.

Rimoli, Laerte (March 1987) "Caminhos para a auto-suficiência." *Revista Brasileira de Tecnológia*. Vol. 18, No. 3.

Rosa, Luiz Pinguelli (1987) "Segurança dos reatores nucleares no Brasil." in Carvalho (ed.), *O Brasil Nuclear*. Porto Alegre: Tche Editora Ltda.

—— (1987) "Anatomia do programa brasileiro." In Joaquim de Carvalho (ed.) *O Brasil Nuclear*. Porto Alegre: Tche Editora, Ltda.

Schmitter, Phillipe (1971) *Interest Conflict and Political Change in Brazil*. Stanford: Stanford University Press.

—— (1974) "Still the century of corporatism?" *Review of Politics* 36.

Schmitz, H., Cassiolato, J.(1992) "Fostering hi-tech industries in developing countries: introduction." In Hubert Schmitz and José Cassiolato (eds) *Hi-tech For Industrial Development*. London: Routledge.

Schmitz, H., Hewitt, T. (1992) "An assessment of the market reserve for the Brazilian computer Industry." In Hubert Schmitz and José Cassiolato (eds) *Hi-tech for Industrial Development*, London: Routledge.

Selcher, Wayne (ed.) (1986) *Political Liberalization in Brazil: Dynamics, Dilemmas, and Future Prospects*. Boulder and London: Westview Press.

Senate Investigating Commission on the Pharmaceutical Industry (November 22, 1988) In *Diário do Senado Federal na Comissão Parlamentar de Inguerito*, Reunião 4.

"Seoul's nuclear fallout." (July 30, 1987) *Far Eastern Economic Review*.

Stepan, Alfred (1978) *State and Society in Peru*. Princeton: Princeton University Press.

—— (1988) *Rethinking Military Politics*. Princeton: Princeton University Press.

Subramanian, R.R. and Mohan, C.R. (1982) "India." In James Katz and Onkar Marwah (eds) *Nuclear Power in Developing Countries*. Lexington, Mass.: Lexington Books.

Tavares, Cristina (1979) "A informática e o controle da sociedade." Text of speech before the Chamber of Deputies, October 17, 1979 (printed in 1985 in *A Informática e a Nova República*. São Paulo: Editora Hucitec.

Tavares, C., and Seligman M. (1984) *Informática: A Batalha do Século XXI*. Rio de Janeiro: Paz e Terra.

"The Nuclear Plan Mushrooms." (July 31, 1981) *Latin American Weekly Report*.

Thomas, Raju (January 1986) "India's nuclear and space programs: defense or development?" *World Politics* 38.

Tigre, Paulo Bastos (1983) *Technology and Competition in the Brazilian Computer Industry*. New York: St. Martin's Press.

—— (1987) *Indústria Brasileira de Computadores: Perspectivas Até Os Anos 90*. Rio de Janeiro: Editora Campus, Ltda.

—— (1988) "Para onde vai a informática?" *Ciência Hoje*, Vol. 8, No. 43.

Tweedale, Douglas L. "Argentina." In Katz, James and Onkar, Marwal (eds) (1982) *Nuclear Power in Developing Countries*. Lexington, Mass.: Lexington Books.

"Uranium jet-nozzle process abandoned." (October 1988) *Modern Power Systems*. Vol. 8.

Viegas, João Alexandre. (March 1987) "Os primeiros passos da autonomia." *Revista Brasileira de Tecnológia*, Vol. 18, No. 3.

Walker, Kenneth N. (1967) "Political socialization in universities." In Seymour Martin Lipset and Aldo Solari (eds) *Elites in Latin America*. New York: Oxford University Press.

Westphal, Larry E. (June 1982) "The private sector as 'principal engine of growth.'" *Finance and Development*, Vol. 19, No. 2.

White, G., and Wade R. (1988) "Developmental states and markets in East Asia: An Introduction." In Gordon White (ed.) *Developmental States In East Asia*. Sussex, England: Macmillan.

Index

144 Index